Home
Is Where
God Calls Us

Dwight L. Short

Home is Where God Calls Us
ISBN 978-0-9845366-0-3

Published by Austin Brothers Publishing
Fort Worth, Texas
www.austinbrotherspublishing.com

Printed in the United States of America

This and other books published by
Austin Brothers Publishing can be purchased at
www.austinbrotherspublishing.com

Austin Brothers
Publishing

A book about
Lodema Short
dedicated
to all of the missionaries
who served with her in the Congo

ENDORSEMENTS FOR
HOME IS WHERE GOD CALLS US

Home is Where God Calls Us is not only a testament of this great mission movement in the Democratic Republic of Congo, but of the author as well. Missionary Lodema Short's call to obedience not only initiated a momentous movement of Jesus Christ over five decades, but also probes that every life that the Lord has created has a redemptive purpose and persuasion. A great story of obedience, courage, and generational discipleship! A great story of author Dwight Short, who as a successful businessmen has impacted the Kingdom of God through the Fellowship of Christian Athletes, financial stewardship, and mission trips to Africa, sharing Christ through athletics and starting orphanages. All can make a difference for Jesus if you blossom right where you are planted.

Joe Abraham
Pastor
Scranton Road Bible Church
Cleveland, Ohio

Christian missionaries the world over have been called by God to focus their energies on developing the gifts and capacities of individuals within the host cultures that welcomed them, thus empowering them, building the church of Christ, and drawing them into the modern era. In this way the missionary movement has been and remains countercultural, quite different in tone and intent from the colonial powers and their successors, which largely sought (and still seek) to extract wealth rather than develop the potential of the indigenous peoples. This view is a needed corrective to much current thought about the relationship between Christian mission and the colonial era, and it is only one of many special insights that can be gleaned from Dwight Short's *Home is Where God Calls Us*. Through the story of Lodema Short of Congo Inland Mission, we learn about the missionary calling and task—its persistence, its power, and its effects. We learn about Congo, a country with enormous potential, which has also lived through intense suffering across its history, and continues to struggle to find its future. Missionaries and mission skeptics, political analysts, nation builders, history buffs, and all those who long for God's kingdom to come in fullness have much to gain in reading this well researched, thought-provoking story. I highly recommend it!"

Rod Hollinger-Janzen
Executive Coordinator
Africa Inter-Mennonite Mission
Goshen, Indiana

I knew Lodema Short during her years on staff at the Nyanga Secondary School. Her excellent classroom teaching is well documented.

However, her most valuable contribution was to the development of faithful Christian men and women. Lodema spent many hours out of the classroom, one on one, mentoring students, helping them understand a lesson, an assignment, or advising them regarding a personal problem.

When students went to her house, for whatever reason, they knew they were going to a counselling session and a prayer meeting, and they loved it.

Earl Roth
Former Director (Principle)
Nyanga Secondary School.

Contents

Acknowledgements

This project has been a two year journey with many people helping by supplying documents, letters, interviews, and editing advice. If you were part of this project and I missed including you on these pages, I ask for your forgiveness as I was the beneficiary of many more people than I could ever have imagined. The numerous interviews that I had in Congo in July, 2012, at the Centennial Celebration included both formal and informal interviews, and each one made a great contribution to the total information we were able to build for this work.

THANK YOU FOR YOUR HELP!!

Wanda Short, Laurel J. Short, and Ted Short, editing, re-writes, and photos; to Jenny & Tim Bertsche for writing the Introduction and to Ruth Keidel Clemens for photos, documents, and of course for writing the Foreword.

A special thanks to John Heese who was a part of the 1960 Evacuation and took many pictures of the events. He had not looked at these slides for many years and asked Brad Graber to help him digitize them. We are all grateful beneficiaries of his efforts to record what happened, and his gracious encouragement to us to share them is appreciated.

One of the students of Lodema who was of utmost value in offering insight was Mutombo M'Panya. Many thanks to him for his efforts to read sections of the book, and help me reflect on multiple aspects of the issues

INTERVIEWS: (Mission, Church, and Family)

Dr. Emanuel Mbualungu
Wayne Short
Jim and Jenny Bertsche
Ted Short
Tim Bertsche
Joyce Short Robarge
Ada Arps
Millie Arnos
Jane Short
Ruth Keidel Clemens
Earl Roth
John Heese
Allan Wiebe
Arnold & Grace Harder
Martini Janz
Rod Hollinger Janzen
Gladys Graber
Sara Regier
Bradley Graber
Rick & Marilyn Derksen
Donna Colbert
Gerald & Marilyn Short
Laurel J. Short
John Lohse
Wanda Short
Matthew Stanard, author of *Selling the Congo*

Congolese Family - Including former students and friends

Theodore Mbualungu - Member of 1958 World's Fair Choir
Sambi Romain Mikasa
Maurice Ilunga - Member of 1958 World's Fair Choir

Kabasele Bantubriado Trudou
Leon Ngandu - Member of 1958 World's Fair Choir
Lodema Short Kanemu (tribute to Lodema)
Mutombo M'panya
Sammy Tshibada
Zachee Mbuya - Member of 1958 World's Fair Choir
Robert Irundu Matundu
Adolphe Komuesa Kalunga
Nowella Kubella
Mado Fumunynga on behalf of her husband Marcel Tshishingue
Jeaun Fumunynga
Sister Bercy Mundedi
Mishambu Lupaya
Pastor Rani Mpango
Paporo Mbamandjare
Julie Katambue
Laurent Kamizehd
Bernard Lola Pulumba
Timothie Mbidikasia Tshibengu
Marcel Ntumbua-wa-Mbuyi
Alidor Tambue KumanKanda
Freddy Ngandjambe
Sister Nyanga Anasthisie Mbidia
Yongo Somi Placide

Most of all, I thank my wife, Marlene who has allowed me the time and space to travel to faraway places to interview countless numbers of people to build the story of this legacy. She has taken care of so many of the things that are often taken for granted, but will never be by me as she has supported this effort to tell about Lodema and all of her work for the Lord.

Foreword

Lying on a blanket on our front porch under the intense Milky Way with my father and siblings, Dad mentioned we may have to leave Congo soon. Two weeks later we quickly packed up what we could take with us, handed the house keys to the pastor, and drove off to join the convoy to Angola. The Independence Movement and associated unrest of 1960 had spilled over to affect the missionaries.

Congolese church leaders advised the missionaries to leave, feeling they couldn't guarantee their protection. Missionaries disagreed whether to stay for the church and their call to serve that church, or to leave for their personal safety. Many Congolese felt abandoned by the evacuation of the missionaries. These events strained the relationship between the missionaries and the Congolese church. At the same time, the church continued to grow and gain some independence as well.

Years later around a pot-luck meal, I listened to missionaries recount tales of evacuation. Lodema's story of leaving her peaceful vacation at Lake Madimape in her high-top fishing boots stole the show!

Like Lodema, my parents (Levi and Eudene Keidel) felt a deep sense of call to work with the church in Congo. My mother sensed a call when she was only nine years old. On their first date she told Levi that she was going to Africa as a missionary nurse, and if he wasn't interested, they may as well drop the relationship right then and there! Over the years Eudene established and supported medical dispensaries and maternity wards. Levi developed a Christian literature distribution system for the Kasai provinces. Together they strengthened church leadership, stationed for several years at Nyanga with Lodema.

Growing up with my parents' strong sense of call, I came to understand that a *call to mission* is not reserved only for the Keidels and the

Lodema's of this world. As Christians, we are all called to participate in God's mission in the world, to love God and love our neighbors. *Call to mission* includes our commitment to family, church, and vocation.

The Mennonite church in Congo has grown to 216,000 members, celebrating its centennial in July 2012. While attending the celebrations in Tshikapa, representing Mennonite Central Committee, it was a joy to speak with many Congolese pastors and lay leaders, men and women who remembered the contribution of missionaries like Lodema. These leaders continue faithfully in their ministry to the Mennonite church in Congo.

Ruth Keidel Clemens

Introduction

Lodema Short gave her life to mission work in Congo, Africa. She came from the Evangelical Mennonite Church in Archbold, Ohio, a very active and supportive church. She had many relatives and friends there who supported her financially and prayed for her regularly.

As I remember Lodema out on the mission station, she served in Education, and was qualified to teach in the Secondary Schools—or High Schools. She taught in the French language. Elementary schools were taught in the local African vernacular, but all higher education was taught in the national language of the Belgian Congo, which is French.

Lodema was an excellent teacher. I heard many Congolese young people speak well of her. They said they learned a lot in her classes, and she explained things well to them. Lodema expected her students to listen and to carry out their assignments. She was good at discipline because she did not tolerate *goofing off* in her classroom. The Congolese students seemed to respect her for this.

Lodema also spent a lot of time teaching the Congolese Men's Choir. This choir was made up of Secondary School students. She trained them to read and sing in four-part harmony. Choosing the best singers from the school, they were prepared to sing at the huge World's Fair in Brussels, Belgium in 1958. They were invited by the Belgium Fair committee to represent the Kasai Region of Congo, and their way was paid by the Belgian government. They turned out to be a very popular feature at the fair, and had additional impromptu invitations to sing at other locations.

Our family was able to attend this Fair on our way back to the United States for furlough. We heard them give a concert, and were so proud of them and the great preparation Lodema had done with them. At the end of the concert our three children ran up to their *friends from Congo* and hugged their legs. The students and the onlookers alike were delighted at this display of affection from small children to friends who reminded them of home!

Lodema Short represents a special cadre of single missionary women who dedicated their lives and careers to service in the Congo. Most every mission station had a house where the *single ladies* lived. They served as teachers, nurses, pharmacists, in literature development and production, health, and cottage industries. Leaving family and friends behind, as well as better prospects for marriage, they served in difficult places of isolation, disease, and sometimes danger. With fatigue and loneliness as their companions, they persevered under Spartan lifestyle conditions in the work and calling to which they were committed.

As the annals of history reveal the work of God's kingdom building in the Congo, the names of Lodema Short and a host of other missionary women will be read with thanksgiving. Gratitude must be expressed for their commitment, their courage, and the selfless dedication they gave to making the name of the Lord Jesus known in the Congo.

Jenny and Tim Bertsche

(Jim and Jenny Bertsche served in the Congo alongside Lodema for many years. Their insights and comments confirm an onsite, first hand witness of activities and events that are central to the themes of this book. Their son, Tim Bertsche, also was born in Congo, and served there as well as other mission callings in other parts of Africa. Jim served as an important confidant to this author in the work of Home is Where God Calls Us. *Without his help and the resources he provided in his books on Congo, this book would not have been possible. We send a special thank you to the Bertsche Family for all they represent in the legacy of this work in Congo and especially for how special they have all been in their support of this publication. Blessings to all of you!)*

Independence From Belgium;
Dependance on God

"Do not lay up for yourselves treasures on earth, where moth and rust consume and where thieves break in and steal, but lay up for yourselves treasures in heaven, where neither moth nor rust consumes where thieves do not break in and steal. For where your treasure is, there will your heart be also." Matthew 6:19-21 (RSV)

The semester was finally over and all the teachers were eager for some rest and relaxation. It was late in June of 1960, and the kids at Lycee Miodi (also known in French as *Ecole Menagerie*) School in Nyanga, of the Belgian Congo, had started their summer vacation, celebrating Independence by declaring school and studying to be unnecessary.

Their expectations for all kinds of wonderful gifts that would accompany *freedom* had reached such proportion that foreign missionaries were not very good sources of information about realistic approaches to the coming changes. The teachers needed a vacation even more than the students, and they had two weeks of glorious down time away from the schools, churches, and clinics that would be perfect for re-charging the batteries and watching the Congo Independence Movement from afar.

Lodema Short had been in the Belgian Congo since 1947, and she had seen many changes and promises of change that had fallen short of helping the Congolese people during her tenure. In fact, the very first of the missionaries who were working in the Kasai region of Congo settled in this part of Africa in 1912, when Lawrence Haigh and his wife Rose were sent from a relatively comfortable farming life in the USA to this remote part of God's creation. What is it that moves people to give up the comforts of home to move families and resources to a place like Congo?

Ironically, the changes that many hoped would make a big difference were in play in that period of time as well. King Leopold II of Belgium had imposed some of the most egregious policies on the people of Congo to line his pockets with unimaginable wealth from the late 1800's through 1908 when the Belgian government took over running the country and imposing restrictions on their own king. New Belgian policies in 1909 opened the country for more freedom, and residents of the Congo were optimistic that this would be a new day and a better day for all of them. Those freedoms proved to be elusive, and in fact the extraction of wealth by the Belgians was only slightly more civilized when compared with King Leopold II. Building schools, hospitals, and churches was mostly ignored by the Colonial power brokers except to encourage mission organizations to do that work for them so they could take the credit.

One example of positive change from 1900 to 1960 was a literacy rate that had improved from less than 10% of the country able to read and write to well over 65% who could now do both. The capital of the country was still known as Leopoldville, named after the monarch King Leopold II of Belgium (talk about how difficult it is to kill a weed) who had pillaged the land and enslaved its people to extract rubber and ivory from 1885 to 1908. It was the closest version of a modern city in the entire country, and by far its largest.

Progress in schools, hospitals, and the villages was primarily due to the efforts of both Catholic and Protestant missionaries while the Belgians happily watched. Leopoldville would someday be renamed Kinshasa, but in 1960 names were the least of importance when all of the country looked at the event of Independence as a combination of freedom, prosperity, and pride. The missionaries believed this could be fool's gold, but they had no idea just how significant the tribal infighting for power in the new version of Congo would change their much needed vacation let alone their lives.

When the missionaries from Lodema's house went on vacation at the end of the 1960 school year, they left their stations behind to enjoy the natural beauty of a country that had everything. Lakes and rivers along with wild animals, jungles, and rain forests that were the envy of naturalists everywhere helped to pass the time when driving on dirt and gravel roads. Such natural beauty is commonplace in the internal expanse of Congo. This doesn't even come close to the beauty of Congo beneath the surface where trillions of dollars of strategic and valuable minerals were lodged. Lodema looked forward to times like this when they could relax, go fishing, share and study the Bible together, and talk about how God had called them to this work.

She even planned ahead to offer being the cook and dish washer the first week of vacation so that she could just fish and reflect on life the second week. Her colleagues quickly accepted her offer and assumed that reversing that schedule was an even better deal for them.

There had been some rumblings around many of the Congo Inland Mission (CIM) stations during the last weeks of school from groups who were anxious to gain a foothold to power when the Belgians left the country and the Congolese took over. For that reason, the missionaries always tried to stay close to short wave radio equipment in case there was any need for communication from central office. Luckily on this vacation, they did not make an exception.

Lake Madimape was more than one hundred miles from Nyanga, and by car or rugged off-road vehicle this would be the better part of a day trip on the roads of Congo. If the roads were needed to get to one of the local diamond mines, you could transverse those roads at much faster speeds. Even the treacherous ferry ride across one of the rivers on the pontoon boats couldn't dampen the enthusiasm for vacationing at this lake which had become a tradition for missionary retreats and gatherings.

Lodema and Sue Schmidt jumped in the car with all their camping gear, wading boots to get closer to the really good fishing, and enough provisions to make the fresh fish taste that much better. It was obvious that many Congolese people were on the move in widely scattered patterns, but this was not that unusual after the end of school as some families were going to a better work location for the summer.

Sue spotted one of her students carrying a gun that she had never known him to possess. She thought he might be going hunting but she also couldn't reconcile that his family could barely afford school fees, and to see him with a gun like that didn't coincide with her impression of the young man and his family's normal patterns. The two women, along with George and Justina Neufeld, would relish getting to the cabins and leaving all of the Independence turmoil behind them... or so they thought as they drove on to Lake Madimape. Lodema was thinking that many of her friends and colleagues from the other mission stations would be on their way to rest and relax with her very soon! Two of her closest friends on the Congo mission field, Lois Slagle and Fanny Schmallenberger, were also on their way to the lake and this promised to be a great time of renewal.

Even the roads seemed more crowded than normal, and on a good day the roads were not easy to make good time. News from friends at the other CIM mission stations was a little tense as other missionaries were also getting their things together to join the women from Nyanga for the vacation at the lake and the long awaited time of renewal. Tensions were mounting from news of conflict and violence that were sifting through rumors and reports from various sources, especially in and around Leopoldville. This had been going on during the buildup and anticipation of Independence. The women drove on to the lake fully thinking that the time to relax and recharge would be welcomed by everyone.

The women talked about their friends and family members from the USA who were always praying for their safety, sending them barrels of supplies, and writing letters on onion skin paper to save weight related postage on the letters that would preferably be sent by airplane rather than by steamship. Communication was delayed by several days even if airmail was used, or weeks at a time if steamship postage was chosen. Discussion about nieces, nephews, brothers, sisters, and parents dominated the time on the road, and were a pleasant diversion to the turmoil going on in the country and the closing of the school year. Writing letters back to family members was also the only way to keep in touch with activities in the Congo, which was always important to those in the states. This vacation time would also allow Lodema to catch up on her correspondence and offer time to write return letters.

Vacations were a great time to catch up and reflect on important news items that were part of the letters received from a recent mail drop from Mission Aviation Fellowship (MAF) Pilots. What a blessing those MAF pilots have been to all of us in Nyanga, they agreed! Their lifeline to the rest of the world seemed to always relate to those daring men who fly single engine aircraft from Leopoldville to everywhere else! Of course, the pickup truck from Nyanga would still have to pick up the airmail in Kikwit each week as the pilots could not take the time to land at all the smaller and obscure villages with the mail. Magazines and bulletins were often six weeks and even six months behind in the news that was being relayed to those who served on the mission stations in a place like Congo.

Lodema was also happy to be facing a rather quiet summer session compared to the past few years. In 1958, she was the chaperone to nine Congolese students who were invited to perform at the Brussels World's Fair in Belgium. This event was certainly one of the highlights of her work in Congo since it displayed for the entire world to see the abilities and potential of her students. The pressure of taking nine young black men from humble origins of the Congo into the heart of European culture carried a special responsibility, and she was not unaware of its significance. The practice and preparation for Brussels was as intense as the trip itself, and the teams of CIM people had all been instrumental in making it a success. Despite the Belgians' efforts to politicize and show symbolic propaganda about the primitive Africans, her students had broken all records for shattering racial opinions.

In 1959, she was chosen to be a leader and delegate to the national conference leaders of the church in Congo. That turned out to be the very last all CIM (meaning all white) missionary conference that was held in Congo, but Lodema and her friends had no idea about that when they left for vacation that day in late June of 1960. The future of the church and Christian outreach in all of Congo was actually hanging in the balance of power in those days. That was impossible to predict when the main focus this day was just to get to the lake and kick back and enjoy some quiet time.

Arriving at the cabins and the surroundings at Lake Madimape for their vacation was a little unsettling. Many of the other missionaries were late in arrival as blocked and crowded roads along with rebel activities were having an even larger impact on other mission stations. They unpacked their things and tried to ready the cabins for all the others so they could get on with their vacation as soon as possible. Suitcases, food, and fishing gear took priority to set up the cabins for the next two weeks.

Had the folks from Mutena arrived first, they could have avoided a lot of extra work and also avoided wasting valuable time in what turned out to be life and death events. The missionaries from close by Mutena had been the last to leave for this event, and fortunately, they had been informed by the CIM leaders that a major change was about to take place. Their short wave radio messages could not have been more dramatic nor could they have been more imperative! George Neufeld was as surprised as anyone to have to deliver this message to the women who had spent so much time prepping the cabins. **"PACK UP WHATEVER YOU CAN AND LEAVE FOR ANGOLA IMMEDIATELY!"**

Anyone who had gone ahead to Lake Madimape was instructed to leave ASAP and told to not return home for anything, but to head to Angola! While the women were concerned about setting up for the others, there was a lot of unrest and violence taking place in Leopoldville. Congolese Independence movements were annoyed that changes were not taking place fast enough; therefore it was time to use tactics more forceful than words. Anyone who happened to be resisting these changes in any way were potentially quick and sudden victims of vigilante politicos and militia leaders who were concerned about tribal retribution and turf wars. Most of all, anyone who was considered complicit in any way with the Belgian authorities became most vulnerable. It was already very late in the day so Lodema's focus changed from setting up for vacation to deciding what should be taken along for the journey to Angola. She started praying for all those who were victims of the violence as well as their own safety.

Confirmation of the violence and turmoil was so strong that the months of preparation for possible emergency procedures were already being enacted. Leaders of the CIM were in prayer with local leaders struggling with the decision whether to evacuate the country or stay and help all the members of their community. They were fearful of being victimized by tribal and ethnic differences that were either taking ground or defending their homelands.

Lodema's closest friends, Jim and Jenny Bertsche, had already decided they were going to stay. This was a big deal because they also had three small children who had all been born on Congolese soil.

When rioting started in 1959 in Leopoldville just a year earlier, CIM leaders feared that similar kinds of unrest and frustration could spread to other areas, including those outlying areas where staff was deployed. The planning for such a time as this was being tested beyond even their worst expectations. Little did the women from Nyanga know that soon they would be in the middle of an evacuation from this very planning. It would not be long before the Bertsche's and all of the CIM staff would be relegated to unwelcome non-Congolese (mostly white) people fleeing the Congo and heading to another country for safety. Within a few hours, over 200 Mennonite Missionaries were leaving their Congolese neighbors and families behind to seek shelter back in their original homes in North America.

It was just over a year later, and the fears of the people were that the leaders with the most guns would fill the void left by the Belgians. The fate of tribal enemies under these new leaders could carry deadly consequences. Many of those same forces were now stirring the pot of violence in the nation's capital, and who could tell if this would spill over to outlying villages and communities such as theirs?

Such was the case in the Kasai region where differences between the Baluba and Lulua tribes was elevating to dangerous levels. CIM authorities were troubled when their village leaders huddled together with them and asked them to keep their mission staff and medical staff on sight for the people who might need them. Meanwhile, cautious leaders, families, and government representatives in Europe and the USA had other plans. Their plan was that all non-Congolese should leave the Congo NOW!

When Christian leaders ask people to step out of their comfort zone and join the Great Commission, they would do well to also remember what happens in developing countries when political weaknesses become victim to hungry and deprived citizens. Lodema and the other missionaries must have been asking themselves how they got into this mess when all they wanted to do is share the love of Jesus Christ with a dying world.

Suddenly, they were struck with their first day of vacation turning into a frighteningly dark night when the others who were supposed to join them were instructed to get in anything that moves and drive as soon as possible the next day to get OUT of the country. DO NOT RETURN HOME, the voice said, and drive as soon as possible to the Angolan border and meet there for further instructions. "*YES, people have been killed and it is impossible to project if violence will spread to all parts of Congo.*" Some of the rebels are targeting any group of people who they think to be complicit with the former ruling Belgian authorities.

No longer did the fishing equipment or who was supposed to do the dishes and cook seem important. These women and their colleagues from other stations were huddled together to pray for the safety of the entire CIM team. This is quite a contrast to praying for rest and recovery from a busy school year.

They could no longer dismiss the stories of missionaries being slaughtered, or their homes being burned to the ground with people still inside. No longer able to think of anything other than their own safety because that was the message being delivered to them, but somehow relying on a God who had blessed them in so many ways before this night. They laid their heads on pillows of uncertainty as to what tomorrow would bring, but trusted that God would provide for their safety during this crisis.

Leaving in the middle of the night was tempting to all the folks who had arrived at Lake Madimape, but they knew that road safety during daylight hours was difficult enough. Everyone agreed to stay off the Congolese roads at night as they were even less safe to travel in the dark. Angola was at least two hundred miles away, and the sooner they could leave the better. Not knowing which roads would be blocked and which roads would have militia that would be friendly to fleeing missionaries, and especially to three white women driving toward another country; they chose to wait and leave in the morning.

As they sat together and talked about their calling, they prayed that God would spare not just themselves but their students and the local families as well. Lodema wondered where the nine young men who were known as the Congo's *Happy Singers* were that night.

The *Happy Singers* had swept people off their feet in Brussels just two years ago, and they seemed so cultured and accomplished because they could speak multiple languages and sing so well. Would they be vulnerable because they had been known in the community as having been to Belgium and that information alone might have gotten them shot by the wrong person with a gun in their hands? The goals of many of the nine men along with hundreds of their fellow students who had outstanding records at the mission schools were hoping to go to medical school, teacher training school, or professional schools. Their dreams of moving into new occupations would set new standards for their families, but now those ideals might have to be put on hold. It was impossible to predict who was safe and who was going to lose their lives in Congo in the coming days. It was like reality setting in to a very narrow space of time, and a challenge to one's faith that most of us never think about.

Tomorrow promised to be a very frightening, hopefully rewarding, and for certain a challenging day for the missionaries leaving Congo! The cross currents in most of our lives rarely becomes so focused on life and death. Maybe they should? Maybe more realistic expectations for Independence would have been helpful in softening this violence. Then again, maybe not! They prayed on these things as they tried to sleep on the only night of their intended vacation. As it turned out, they might not be observing the Independence movement of Congo from afar, they might just be right in the middle of it all unless they could get to Angola. By this time, the Bertsche's decided that God did not want them to stay in Congo either so they too were packing emergency items to make the journey to Angola with the others to return to the USA or Canada.

Soon the caravans would try to unite and move together once everyone got to Angola. For now, each person wondered if this is where God would allow their life on earth to end as a martyr or a casualty of Congolese Independence. Driving to an unknown area of a distant country on roads that were quickly filling up with often unfriendly and perhaps equally frightened soldiers would be a test of faith. Lodema could only keep repeating one of her favorite Scripture passages, I Thessalonians 5:23-24 (NIV):

"May God himself, the God of peace, sanctify you through and through. May your whole spirit, soul and body be kept blameless at the coming of our Lord Jesus Christ. The one who calls you is faithful and he will do it."

As Lodema laid her head on the pillow and pulled her sleeping bag around her, she wondered what in the world they would do when they did get to Angola? All the talk about leaving as soon as possible and not returning to Nyanga to get any of her personal things was just taking hold in her mind. Nyanga may be out in the middle of a desolate area of the Congo, but that is **HOME!** "Why can I not go back to my home? Why can we not return to the happy days when all of the members of our missionary family in Nyanga enjoyed a good meal, lots of laughs, and everyone's company? Will we all make it home?"

Lodema on the far left enjoying an after meal time of fun with the Bertsche's; the Rocke's; and Entz's all while stationed in Nyanga. (Photo from Wanda Short)

Survival and Returning to the USA

"Blessed are the peacemakers, for they shall be called sons of God." Matthew 5:9 (RSV)

There was mostly silence and prayers as the cars moved away from Lake Madimape. This retreat was supposed to be a reward vacation after a challenging school year for the teacher missionaries from the Kasai Region of the Belgian Congo. June was almost over, and it seemed like months since school had let out, yet it was just a little more than a week ago when they were closing up the Lycee Miodi School in Nyanga for summer vacation.

"Do you think maybe we are overreacting by evacuating all of us?" one of the women wondered.

June was disappearing quickly as they had wasted time traveling from Nyanga to Lake Madimape, and now they are back on the road again heading south to Angola under great uncertainty as to what may lie ahead. The summer vacation time may be consumed in all of this driving around! They all agreed that perhaps a little

Leaving Charlesville mission station to head to Angola. (Photo by John Heese, edited Brad Graber)

time in Angola while all of this unrest blew over and they might just return to their stations for the start of school in the fall. But what to do in the meantime in Angola? It turns out they were not welcomed by the Portuguese colonial rulers since they feared their presence might start a revolution in Angola.

Driving to Angola was not a common strategic or vacation destination since there was not much to do in that part of Africa compared to many other options. However, today was a critically different situation. CIM missionaries and other evacuees were feverishly driving south to escape the violence of tribal militia groups. Did we not serve a God who is *big* enough to protect us even in times of turmoil such as this, they wondered.

The idea of staying to help out in any way possible kept creeping into the conversation. In Lodema's heart of hearts, she was feeling like she was leaving *home* rather than going *home*! She trusted the CIM leaders because of their long track record of doing what is right in the sight of God, but in her inner most thoughts she worried that

CIM missionaries connect short wave radio to generator to contact home office in Elkhart, Indiana to give progress report on their evacuation journey from Congo to Angola while on the road out of Congo (photo by John Heese, edited Brad Graber)

their fleeing from Congo might be attracting more danger than if they stayed and helped the people from each of their villages.

Jim and Jenny Bertsche were having similar misgivings about leaving the Congo. Confronting each other on the steps to their attic, Jenny asked Jim, "Why are we abandoning our family here in Congo when they need us the most?"

He could not answer her because he had the very same concern. The attic was where their long term food and provisions were kept, and as they scrambled to take provisions for a journey they didn't really want to be part of, they continued to pray, to seek, and to hear God's directions.

The Bertsche's were a married couple who both shared the vision for calling and ministry in Congo. This is often a problem for the wives of husbands who feel called to go to a mission station but the women share neither the calling nor the need to leave family and comforts to take on a position in a faraway place. Evacuations and stress like this will bring out all such fault lines, but none of those seemed to appear during this time for them. It was still early in the process of mobilizing two hundred people to leave the dangerous situation, but the questions kept being raised to heaven from the hearts of the leaders and colleagues of the entire mission community.

STAY OR GO?

Many were prepared to die there if that was God's will, but perhaps they were to be a witness to others in showing proper caution by leaving now to then return another day. Their children seemed confused about the need to be leaving Congo, but they too were ready for an adventure if that was what Angola was all about. Lodema could tell by now that her fellow missionaries also felt like they were leaving their home (Congo), not returning to their homes (USA).

Word of this evacuation was spreading like wildfire, and especially among the families of the missionaries back in North America. Some family members would be adamant that they would never want their relatives to return to such a dangerous place, and they just prayed for them to be safe and get away from such a violent environment.

Belgian authorities had hoped for a quiet, peaceful transfer of power, but their military and police forces were badly outmanned by Congolese forces that wanted every aspect of Belgian influence expelled! Instead of expulsion, even more troops were being flown in to try to protect Belgian nationals who were unsure if they should stay to protect farms and businesses they had spent a lifetime to build. The United Nations was also helping the Belgians and any foreigners who were in danger of being swept up in the violent fever of Independence.

Driving along what used to be quiet roads, the missionary women could tell that there were already winners and losers in this battle for power. The losers were being forced from their homes and were fleeing on foot to find a place for their families that could provide safety, even if the idea of comfort would not exist for some time. The *winners* would often show power in the form of weapons and a uniform that would be a second hand military camouflage shirt that was probably taken from either a corpse or a prisoner.

Jim Bertsche discusses options with other families. Even as the caravan was forming to go to Angola, there was constant prayer and discussion as to whether this was God's will for them to be leaving. (Photo by John Heese, edited Brad Graber)

They had driven quite a few miles, and mostly they saw village residents walking on the roads along with those who were obviously displaced. It was several hours into their journey south when their first confrontation took place with a militia group. These particular soldiers were new at this sort of thing, and their politeness was both hilarious and welcomed. Ten US dollars from each vehicle and then the evacuees were allowed to move on toward Angola! What a business!

Young boys who were carrying guns and blocking the roadways so they could control, intimidate, and of course collect money for passage, would become a common obstacle in leaving Congo to get to Angola. Belgian currency was usually most acceptable, but today, the only currency would be prayer and US Dollars, in that order.

Speaking Tshiluba and knowing the dialect of the young men demanding payment also did not hurt along with a few crisp dollar bills. Fifty miles down and still more than one hundred sixty to go

Trying to make time on Congolese roads is not easy. Despite the dangers and violence all around them, the missionaries had to stop to transfer fuel for the cars and to allow the kids to stretch their legs. Levi Keidel (dark bibs) and his family give thanks for the progress they have made to this point in the evacuation. (Photo by John Heese, edited Brad Graber)

for the evacuees and an unknown number of makeshift road blocks by newly crowned toll road pirates still to be negotiated. Lodema and her colleagues were still feeling some familiarity because they had lived in this region long enough that many people recognized them from the schools in Nyanga and Tshikapa.

What if they ran out of dollars before they got to Angola? What if they didn't have enough money to satisfy each of these vigilante groups who were using the cover of Independence to extort money from all of those folks who were fleeing the area? As it turned out, four of these *toll booths* from the jungle were all that slowed them down, and fortunately they had enough US dollars to appease their armed guardians of the roadways.

Word had spread that there was a caravan of vehicles that left from the mission station in Kalonda near Tshikapa, and all the missionaries were to try to join that caravan. This would have been easy had Lodema and several others not left early to go to Lake Madimape as they would have been in the middle of the group leaving from Kalonda.

Training to be a missionary at Moody Bible Institute during World War II was full of great courses and marvelous professors of the Word, but none of the courses included how to handle drunk soldiers and power crazed tribal leaders. Lodema even reflected on how she had spent time in Belgium learning all the rules of how to live in a colony governed by a distant European country. The colonization course designed by the Belgian authorities was intended to build allegiance from all the missionaries toward Brussels. Those courses did nothing to prepare for this day however. European superiority and the advantages of colonization were themes that suddenly seemed both passé and also loaded with false bravado.

There had always been two types of missionaries in the minds of the Belgian government; domestic (meaning Catholic) and foreign (meaning Protestant). For many years, the Belgians only offered financial support to Catholic missionaries, and they were considered the first team in Congo. Over time, it became obvious that a whole variety of Protestant mission groups such as Baptist, Presbyterian, Methodist, Lutheran, and of course the Mennonites were doing significant work in Congo, and the Belgians decided they needed to have some influence with them as well. The Belgian Authorities decided to offer the Protestant Missionaries a course that would teach them about the history of Colonial rule in Congo, and when completed provide financial support for each graduate. That course work that each missionary studied in Brussels and Antwerp may have provided welcome financial support; but they never talked about how to leave a country when under siege.

All of Lodema's training, and even the financial support the Belgians subsequently gave to foreign missionaries, was not going to be helping much today as she and all the CIM people scrambled for safety. The more they could distance themselves from the Belgian Colonial Authorities the less likely they would be to trigger the wrath of Congolese militias that were forming as they were heading to Angola. This close connection between the Belgian colonialists and the missionaries may have also contributed to the perception that the missionaries were one and the same as the colonialists, and needed to leave the country as well. With such short notice to make decisions about "do we stay or do we go," this association must have weighed heavily on the missionary leadership.

The propaganda that was meted out in those same courses also had a poignant appearance when looked at through the lens of people who had been long time victims of economic deprivation. Little did these scrambling missionaries know that future dictators and leaders in an Independent Congo would institute policies that would further such deprivation. This day was not the best time to think or reflect on history. Just get to Angola and reunite with the other CIM team members and go from there.

Just as these reflections were going through her thoughts, a military jeep with several armed men passed their car and forced them off of the road. There were just two cars in Lodema's little caravan, and the soldiers pulled the men out of the cars first and slammed them up against the side of the jeep! The soldiers demanded to know where they were going! The men stayed calm and started repeating scripture inside their hearts.

There was not much discipline in this militia group, and finally after several minutes of berating and badgering, George Neufeld asked the young man if he could speak? "We are peace loving people and in fact we have worked with many of your family and neighbors at the Nyanga schools to teach you to read, write, and understand the Bible."

This not only stopped the shouts from the soldiers, but they realized that they spoke clearly in the Tshiluba language. Most Belgians would never bother to learn local tribal languages as these missionaries clearly had done.

Lodema and the other women were praying with their eyes and ears wide open! They had heard horror stories about women being raped and abused by soldiers on other mission stations, and confrontations such as this could easily elevate into such unthinkable happenings.

George told the soldiers, "We may be leaving for Angola, but we promise to come back and resume our work here in Congo if you will let us! Our leaders believe this is the best course of action for us right now and we will pray for your safety during this time as well as ours."

George offered to pay for their gas to keep peace on the roadways. He later wondered why he offered to pay for gas. The Holy Spirit gave him those words because the odor of a bribe accompanies a dishonest transaction, and George tried to keep these young men's dignity along with the safety of those in his care. It was only six missionaries and family members, but you could not convince these six people that God was not in their midst.

By now, prayer groups and vigils had been formed in Lodema's home church in Archbold, Ohio. Family members were praying in their homes as word started to emanate from CIM headquarters in Elkhart, Indiana, that orders had been given that all missionaries were to leave Congo and rendezvous in Angola, and wait there for further instructions on the next steps to be taken.

Lodema was already concerned about how much this would frighten her older brothers, Laurel and Fred, their wives, Marjory and Jeanette, and each of their family members. Her younger sister Isabelle, her husband Louie also worried from afar as word reached all of them in various stages that Lodema was in harm's way in a distant land that none of them could fully understand.

The US family members all remembered the commissioning services and the sweet sounds of music and the words of dedication that may have mentioned danger, but no one ever expects this under the watchful eye of a loving God. But all of that was now being muffled and suppressed by the thought of one of the sweetest people that God had ever placed on earth possibly being abused, and perhaps even dying a martyr's death.

Their understanding of the violence and unrest was restricted to the news on television and limited coverage about the Belgian Congo in the national newspapers. When scenes appeared of missionaries being killed in areas near Kinshasa, the family members could only imagine that the people they were reporting on could be one of their loved ones! Providentially, the women of Nyanga and none of the AIMM/CIM missionaries experienced such violence. The greatest testament to God's grace was that all of the CIM Missionaries would be able to return home unharmed.

Washing up at the river on the Congo/Angola border, as Angolan children watch from the bridge. We were very dusty after driving all night. Perry had been ill so my mother was eager to get us cleaned up. From left to right: Eudene Keidel, Pete Buller (bending behind Eudene), Levi Keidel (bending in the river), Paul Keidel (walking down the hill), Jim Peters (MCC PAX), Charles Buller (small child behind Jim), Priscilla Keidel, Gladys Buller. On the top of the hill are Ruth Keidel, Jeannette Buller, Perry Keidel behind Jeannette), James Buller. (Commentary provided by Ruth Keidel Clemens, picture is from her father, Levi Keidel's archives)

The next set of militia types that the women from Nyanga en-countered turned out to be central government troops that were sym-pathetic to their needs to get to the Angola border. Even though they had not crossed over the border, there was a sense that they could exhale and not feel the blood rushing from their brain. These men did not extort money from them, but they were clear that the sooner the women moved along to the next country up the road the better. One of the soldiers walked over to the car to see who was inside as each of the women felt their hearts pumping so hard they could feel the *cloth of their dresses next to their heart moving in the same rhythm as their blood stream.* They had past the other road blocks successfully, but now the soldier motioned to open the window!

"Momma Kanemu, is that you?" he asked.

"Kabasile Mikasa, is that you?" Lodema replied back.

"You need to move on to Angola," he said, and reached out his hand in both love and concern.

"We are headed that way for sure and it hurts us to have to leave right now when we know so many people are hurting."

He re-iterated to Lodema that he and her students would always remember the lessons she had taught them, and especially the truths of God's Word. Even at a time like this, teachable moments were everywhere, and the seeds of power, greed, and jealousy would be in competition with kindness, generosity, and understanding. Which fruits of the spirit would emerge?

Once again, communicating in the native language of Tshiluba or Giphende was key to the military men's sympathies for those in haste to depart the Congo. Most of them could not remember a Belgian of-ficial who spoke their language.

The women paused for a second to thank God for a friendly face on the road to Angola that day. His words about the importance of the lessons he had learned would never depart from their pounding hearts. The kindness he showed, even when he could have extracted more money from the women since he was in a position of power would also not soon be forgotten.

A country like Congo had so long been dominated by outside colonizers that the roots of graft and fraudulent behavior ran like a giant river through the entire continent of Africa. Many years later, law enforcement is still almost impossible to control, and only the basic instincts of human fairness allow for the civility that does exist. They would never see Mikasa again, and many years later they would wonder what had happened to him.

This journey took many more days than expected. Moving more than two hundred people in caravan along dusty roads became a logistical nightmare. Taking bathes became a major consideration for sanitary and safety issues. What to do with the vehicles once they reached Angola's capital, Luanda?

Many thankful prayers were rendered over the next several days for the efforts of the Catholic and Methodist Missionary Societies for planting mission stations in Angola. In addition to the entire CIM mission staff and families, there were many other cars filled with Belgian and European evacuees who had no idea where they were going or how they would get there.

They found a Catholic Mission station in the Angolan bush country that had been suggested by a friendly trucker who had helped them through some rough and muddy terrain. The CIM missionaries had brought considerable food, but the trip was not conducive to stopping long enough to prepare food or meals. The mission had huge papaya and the canned foods made for a most welcome meal. They prayed and invited the Belgian evacuees to eat first. Lodema and several other single women were allowed to sleep in the priest's quarters. She declared the next morning that, "it was the first time she had ever slept in a priest's bed!"

Refreshed by a good night's sleep, they soon pressed on to a Methodist Mission house in Kesuwa, Angola. Through fragmented calls to the USA, the leaders indicated that CIM officials were adamant that the missionaries would not be returning to Congo. Staying several days in Kesuwa with curtains of cloth separating families in the vacant school building confirmed that they would have to press on to Luanda.

Portuguese authorities wanted these pilgrims out of their country too before the local Angolans might get the idea that driving foreigners out of their country might be a good idea.

As it turned out, some missionaries and many Belgians lost their lives during that period of time, and the struggle for Independence had only just begun. Behind these scenes, many Congolese tribal leaders would try to exert power at the highest levels to take over the country. While there was fighting inside of Congo for power, the world's super powers, including the United States, Britain, Russia, China, and of course Belgium, were all trying to force their own agendas on the best outcome for their interests. Controversy still surrounds whether the US Central Intelligence Agency (CIA) helped to orchestrate the installation of eventual dictator Joseph Mobutu along with the assassination of populist Patrice Lumumba. Those events transpired much later, but on this day, survival and safety were of utmost importance.

It was determined that if they drove two more days from Kesuwa that they could reach a railhead in Malanga, Angola. Most of the group, including Lodema, boarded a train to Luanda and awaited further instructions. The ten vehicles that carried all of the people were driven to Luanda separately, and they would park them at another Methodist Mission house in Luanda. One of the first projects for the early returnees to Congo in 1961, would be to organize drivers and mechanics to bring the vehicles back to Congo for use at the various mission stations.

As for Lodema and all the CIM staff, they arrived unharmed in Angola, and within a few days most boarded a United Nations aircraft that had carried foodstuffs for refugees into Congo, to take them back to Europe to then board flights to return to their homes. The US ambassador to Congo requested that all of the American Air Force planes that had the ability to carry passengers in their empty planes to go to Angola and pickup as many missionaries and evacuees as possible. This took several days, and the Methodist Mission House in Loanda went through a lot of pork and beans feeding the Congolese evacuees.

Rail head at Malanga, Angola, missionary families and individuals wait for train to Luanda. (Picture from Ruth Keidel Clemens from archives of Levi Keidel)

After hours of waiting at the Malanga railhead, everyone was able to board the train for the day's journey to Luanda and await further instructions on their next steps toward "home." (Photo by John Heese, edited Brad Graber)

For eight year old Brad Graber, he had endured sleeping on the ground for ten days, fearing that one night lions were in the area of their camp; and only taking baths in the rivers and lakes until arriving at a mission house in northern Angola. Of course, the rest of his siblings, Stan 11, Carolyn 9, Emily 6, and Jeanette 4 had survived as well. Father Harold Graber and his mother Gladys had also used their gifts of the Tshiluba language to express their love and concern to gun toting soldiers to convince them that they were friends who had come in peace and would try to return when possible to continue teaching and working in the local village's schools. They too were granted passage from confrontations with militias and road blocks because they had no weapons other than the Word of God and the Holy Spirit to direct their speech.

Brad's reward, along with all the other missionary families, was to board a giant, chilly Globemaster 124C in Luanda after it had dropped off food and supplies in Congo. Normally these planes were used for hauling cargo or troops, but this day, they carried Christian Soldiers who found themselves between homes, not sure if they had left home or were going home. Almost everyone got the Globemaster flight experience as they took the evacuees to a US Air Force base in southern France, and then found commercial flights back to the USA and Canada from Paris. Missionary blankets came in handy as many huddled for warmth, and those who could not fit would try to get close to heating pipes in the planes.

Lodema and others landed at an airbase in France about an hour from Paris, and they quickly boarded a bus for deGaulle Airport. Traffic was busier than usual along the roads to the airport, and it took longer than expected to get there. The plane was even pushed back from the boarding area when they arrived. Word of their plight was relayed to the pilots and they stopped the plane to make sure they could board. Watching luggage being rushed along the ground to the plane also became a matter of prayer. When on board, there were several Jewish businessmen on board who decided to take an offering for the families. Most of them had no money at all by this time, but the gener-

The US Air Force and the United Nations organized the empty C-130's to carry people out of Angola and back to Europe after dropping off either troops or food in the troubled areas of Congo. The CIM staff and family members gladly boarded a faster mode of transportation. (Photo by John Heese, edited Brad Graber)

ous gesture allowed each family and individual to get off the plane in New York City with twenty-six dollars.

As Lodema stepped onto the terra firma of Ohio soil at Toledo Express Airport that day in July, 1960, there was great relief. Her family and friends on this side of the Atlantic Ocean could feel a sense of relief. She didn't look at all like she had been through the dangerous episode of her drive from Congo to Angola, and in fact, she thought it was a shame that she had to come home at all. She was just coming into greater awareness that many of the people in other Congo mission stations had not been so fortunate. She couldn't remember where she left her fishing boots nor could she remember what may have been left behind at Lake Madimape.

It turns out that she was also blessed to not have returned to her mission station in Nyanga because many of the militia groups had taken over those compounds and made them into their command headquarters. Luckily for the CIM leadership, they would find most of their compounds to be in better shape than other mission stations, and would start to prepare for reopening as many of them as possible. Surprisingly, for all those greeting Lodema and the other evacuees, many of these very same missionaries would return to Congo much faster than any of them would have guessed on *that day*.

Even the CIM leadership did not expect to return so quickly. They told almost everyone that they should find other work and other things to do for now and they would advise when conditions changed to warrant considering a return to Africa. Those were harsh words to reconcile for Lodema as she knew in her heart of hearts that God had clearly called her to be a teacher in the Congo. Why, oh why was she back in Archbold, Ohio? How soon could she possibly imagine returning to Nyanga, where most people would never think of going, but for her was where God was calling her? She could not imagine that God's calling would change on the whims of rebellions and regime changes.

It took a few weeks to adjust back to living in the USA, but after much prayer and the support of family and friends, Lodema decided to move on. Or, so she thought at the time. There was a teaching job open in Swanton, Ohio, and the chance to complete her bachelor and master's degrees at Bowling Green State University seemed like a good way to sink back into American life.

Driving every day to school in Swanton, and then on to BGSU, gave her time to think about all the children and people back in Congo. It had only been two years earlier that she accompanied nine *Happy Singers* from Congo to the Brussels World's Fair. Where were those young men? Had they been forced to join militia groups or worse yet, been associated with the Belgians to the point of being harassed or even killed?

Would she ever see them again? Her daily prayer was that God would allow her to return to Nyanga to teach both girls and boys to be young women and men and grow in God's love and grace! Were they safe? Did the students and families of Nyanga survive the hostilities that took place there and would the Miodi School still be standing? How would this all turn out?

Better yet, how did she get to this place in life that she felt split between two places so far apart in miles, and even farther apart in culture? How indeed could she deal with the fact that she was **home** but yet she didn't feel she was really **home**? Lodema was starting to understand that **home** is wherever God wants us to be. Not where we are born or where our earthly family resides, but where God's Family resides. Where indeed would that place be for her?

As traumatic and treacherous as the journey was for Lodema and the CIM mission staff and families had been, there were so many others who were not as fortunate during this time. The US government and the United Nations took actions that became controversial as it appeared to only favor Western interests. Their efforts to provide safety for the mission families of the CIM during the evacuation will never be controversial for the people who were evacuated through Angola.

The Congolese citizens who were victimized by the circumstances of these times had to endure severe violence. Tribal differences from hundreds of years would boil over into turf wars and militia conquests. Women and children were the greatest victims of these violent acts as the combination of rape, intentional starvation, and murderous executions became too common. Yes, the decision to leave was difficult and will forever remain a point of contention among many people, but the fact that all the CIM missionaries were spared this violence was an incredible answer to prayer.

There were a bevy of newspaper reporters anxious to talk with the now famous American refugees who had just landed on American soil in New York. Most of the missionaries were beyond their patience and tried to avoid any contact with the newspeople so as not to give the wrong impression.

As happy as they were to be safe at **home**, they were much more exhausted from the two weeks of unexpected travel and hardship. Most of their comments were to say *Thank You* to the United States Air Force and the United Nations flight teams who had been instrumental in helping them leave Africa and eventually return to the US. Some of the families were able to board trains to return to Midwestern states, and others like Lodema boarded flights that would eventually connect back to their families. For Lodema, this meant she would fly into the newly opened Toledo Express Airport in Toledo, Ohio. Welcome Home!

There were many people who celebrated Lodema's return to the United States. Reporters from the *Toledo Blade* were on hand when they disembarked at Toledo Express Airport. Questions about the dangers of their journey were on everyone's mind as they tried to relax after two weeks of scrambling on the back roads of Africa and flying home on military and commercial airplanes.

WS SECTION

BLADE

PAGE 9

RDAY, JULY 23, 1960

Northwestern Ohio Missionaries Home From Congo

—Blade Photos

LODEMA SHORT, Archbold, has been an instructor in a teacher training school in the Congo since 1947.

AFTER 12 days of travel from their stations in the Congo by truck and military and commercial aircraft, two Mennonite missionaries from northwestern Ohio returned to Toledo Express Airport yesterday to be greeted by relatives and friends. Lois Slagle, Pioneer, a nurse in the Congo for 15 years, is shown as she was welcomed by her mother, Mrs. Ada Repp, left; her brother, Herbert Repp and his daughter, Cindy, all of Pioneer.

Traffic Crash Churns Huge Milkshake

They were unharmed and all of the missionaries from the Mennonite mission stations from Congo had been safely returned to their families. The irony of this moment was not lost on the fact that the school that hired Lodema for the start of the 1960 school year in Swanton, Ohio, was less than five miles away from where this picture was taken at the Toledo Airport. (Note *Today's Chuckle* in the newspaper clip)

It would also be a shock to many people when just two years from when they landed, Lodema and Lois would be boarding another plane to return to Nyanga and seek out God's calling for where to find their next **home**! It would be back in the same mission schools in the heart of Congo that then would find their country following a new name, Zaire.

Independence Congolese Style

"Is it not your passions that are at war in your members? You desire and do not have; so you kill. And you covet and cannot obtain; so you fight and wage war..."
James 4:1-2 (RSV)

The summer of 1960 had so many stories at so many different levels that it is impossible to share all of them in a single book let alone just this chapter in Lodema's journey. While the CIM missionaries were integrating back into life in the USA, life for the students of Nyanga, Kalonda, Mukedi, and all of the various mission stations was anything but normal. Even the leaders of CIM who stayed behind to take care of business before returning to the US found themselves in very precarious positions.

One of the most dangerous tasks was to find a safe place for all the money that had been gathered together from the CIM outposts. Prior to their fleeing from Congo to Angola, leaders took all the money from the safes and hid it among two different couriers for safe keeping.

The fighting and violence within the country centered on two primary issues, power and tribal fears. Some of the tribal problems had been created and even exacerbated by the Belgian Colonial authorities. If they could keep some tension between the various tribal groups, it deflected away from their need to maintain control. This division also helped to prevent the same groups from uniting against the Belgians. When the Belgians left a void of security and control in the country, power hungry tribal leaders and opportunists were eager to fill it. Sometimes, this was a combination of wanting to take control of regional areas and bring payback and restitution for past wars and battles.

In other instances, it was the opportunity to take advantage when outside influences provided guns and weapons as a tradeoff for protection to acquire valuable resources in the future. The United States and their European allies were among those outside influences who would seek to invoke their self-interests to continued access to strategic and valuable mineral resources. The Russians and Chinese Communist governments were also trying to play a role in becoming allies with whoever would emerge as the leader of the Congolese territories.

Everyone was thinking of protecting or establishing their turf, and there was no precedent for who was right in this movement so the rush to be in charge was full speed ahead. Belgian authorities had some ideas that this might quiet down and they would be able to re-emerge as the power broker for their former colony. Many businesses, including the largest banks, also thought they would weather the storm and try to stay in the Congo. The Belgians sent troops to protect their citizens and the United Nations sent food and troops to protect everyone else. This neutrality was ambiguous at times as the UN became a surrogate for Western interests both in the expression of humanitarian relief and in the protection of immigrant people who were still in Congo. There was also evidence that weapons made their way to *friendly* tribal leaders via the bags of rice and flour. Somehow, war glorifies the fact that we are all sinners, and there was plenty of evidence of this in Congo.

All the missionaries from Congo Inland Mission made it to safety to Angola, and most of them boarded UN planes to Germany and parts of Europe to then return to North America. To this very day, all the travelers who evacuated from Congo have vivid memories of the Globe Master aircraft that had no seats and no compression controlled cabin since it was a cargo plane that most of the missionaries boarded in Luanda, Angola. Yes, there were benches along the sides of the aircraft that were usually used by military personnel, and the makeshift blanketed areas were actually quite comfortable compared to the ground many had been sleeping on while driving the back roads of Congo and Angola.

But Alan Wiebe and Art Janz along with their spouses decided to stay back for the time being and take care of an important business item. When the word came that all were to leave Congo, one of the leaders in each mission station cleaned out the cash box and brought it along in the evacuation. All this cash (estimates are that they were carrying $14,000 to $17,000) that they had brought with them from the mission stations was burning a hole in their pockets, and their fears of being caught by the wrong people while carrying these large sums of money around was not without merit.

Upon hearing that the Belgian banks were going to remain open, it got them thinking that they could somehow get back to Kinshasa and deposit the money there for safe keeping. This would allow them to have access to the funds when the violence and turmoil subsided and also keep them from walking around with tens of thousands of dollars in their pockets. Based on 2013 dollars, this deposit represented what would be more than two hundred, fifty thousand US dollars.

Their plan was to fly from Angola to Brazzaville and cross over into Kinshasa by ferry boat long enough to hit the Bank of Belgium, make a deposit, and then follow the rest of the team back to the USA. If this seems strange to those of us today who can view this picture from the perfect lens of history, it is beyond shocking that anyone would trust a bank in a developing country like this in the middle of a violent and volatile period. The truth is, it was a stroke of genius as it was just a few months and a few years later that this money would provide the support for reopening the mission stations again. Once they made the deposit, they were able to find safety in UMH (United Mission House) for a few days to then figure out how to return to their North American homes.

The Janz's were originally from Manitoba, Canada, so Art decided to see if some of his fellow Canadians could help them get back home. Most of the other CIM missionaries had taken UN planes to airbases in Europe and then commercial flights back to the states. The Canadian authorities were not very helpful at first as no one was allowed to be on those flights other than military personnel. Yes, the planes were empty and seemed like a good idea, but there was no protocol or authorization for such use.

Finally, the Canadian Ambassador told Art that if the four of them showed up at the air base the next day and pleaded their case directly to the pilots and crews that were unloading the food supplies, maybe they could work something out. There would be no manifest with their names or any listing of their whereabouts, and no official record of their being on any flight, but the next day they flew from Kinshasa to the Ontario Air Force Base courtesy of the Royal Canadian Air Force. Who says we don't serve a big God?

While the missionaries were returning to their homes in North America or the remnant force was at work protecting the scarce funds from the mission stations, many of the Congolese were going through the first phase of Independence. Your life could be in danger if you were a white person, especially if you were a Belgian.

Worse than that, your life was in danger if you were from the Lulua tribal heritage in Baluba territories, and vice versa. The struggle for Independence was now punctuating long standing tribal differences, and if the leadership and control of an area was established by a rival tribal leader that meant all the homes and property of those who were of different origins would be in jeopardy.

Many of the students from the school in Nyanga found themselves and their families in the middle of this turmoil as well. Their time at the boarding school was like an oasis in life as most of their family and friends were not able to attend a school like Miodi Lycee. Each time they returned to family and home, they realized how privileged they were to have teachers like Lodema and people from the mission stations that truly cared about them as much as their families did.

Now many of these kids who had been talking about how great it was going to be when Independence came found themselves traveling by foot to a new *home*. Cities like Tshikapa and Mbuji Mayi where there were significant mining interests were also the focus of power struggles and conflicts with the former Belgian authorities. The mission schools had been a safe place through all the years for children and young people from different tribal origins to study and grow together, now that was being tested.

The new version of the local military and police forces were nothing more than those who grabbed for power first. Holding on to that power was not easy, and so the threat and paranoia about challengers to the positions of authority were everywhere. Young people in Congo were used to what we would call a difficult life of survival and living off the land. But the addition of violence, corruption, and abuse that they could see right in front of them was a life changing event.

It was not unusual to hear about or even see both hangings and executions by gun fire. United Nations peace keepers could affect the law and order in parts of Kinshasa and in some other cities, but the countryside and bush areas were the domain of the tribal warlords who filled that gap. Would there ever be a place for missionaries to return and call this new country soon to be known as Zaire, their home? Would the country itself be better for having forged Independence rather than remaining a colony of Belgium?

With the luxury of history on our side to tell this story, more than fifty years after Independence, it is still clear that Congolese leaders have padded their own bank accounts with little or no regard to the needs of the people of Congo. It is also clear that much of the source for these bribes has come from Western Countries and their Corporations. One of the early leaders, Patrice Lumumba, was considered a popular man of the people, but he was assassinated and removed from office. One of his own men, Sese Seko Mobutu (formerly known as Joseph Desire Mobutu) along with help from the CIA, masterminded this killing.

Mobutu remained in dictatorial power for more than thirty years, and after a brief period of giving lip service to building the Congolese infrastructure, he devoted the vast majority of his time in power to remaining in power and building his own fortune. His accumulated wealth was difficult to measure since he purchased homes and real estate all over the world. Hundreds of millions of dollars would not begin to quantify this thievery. Western complicity helped to prop him up during this time and set a precedent for bribes and self-interest above the needs of the people and the country. That condition still exists in many parts of Congo to this day.

The average Congolese did not fare so well in the new era of Independence. During the summer of 1960, many of the students and families experienced their own evacuation when they were forced to flee their homes simply because they were of the wrong tribal ancestry. For those who did not comply, there were public executions, and homes would be burned with people still in them who refused to leave. Some were arrested who just happened to be in the wrong place when soldiers who were trigger happy wanted to arrest someone to show off their new found power. The jails were overloaded with real prisoners and those who did nothing wrong and should not have been there. If a family member could not pay the ransom to bail them out, many were simply executed to make space for more prisoners.

The greatest risk in this first year of Independence would come from being Belgian and still being in the Congo. Many were still working for the mining companies and businesses that related to mining and construction. The companies themselves tried to hire their own militias but this did not keep the employees from harm's way when they tried to go home at night after work. It turns out that the Congo mining industry represented the source of greed and extortion that would line the pockets of politicians and tribal warlords for many years.

One of the greatest tragedies of any country's history is that of Congo in that the vast resources that have been and still are in the ground there, still have not benefited the general society. The inability to translate that wealth back into infrastructure, schools, hospitals, and recreational facilities is still a blight on the Congo.

But the greatest blight of all is the loss of human talent and dignity. Lodema and the missionaries of Congo could see the talent, the vibrancy, and the spirit of the people of Congo. They saw that when given an education and an opportunity, there was great achievement and excellence. What have we missed in the world today by the doctors, teachers, musicians, and all the potential professionals that have been thwarted in their development by government policies and corporate greed that has left them behind? Lodema saw this potential in every student who was in every class she taught. Lodema saw this in the church as she watched the growth of Pastors who were given an opportunity to attend the Bible Institutes in Tshikapa and Kalonda, and could break the Bread of Life for their fellow man.

Pastor Adolphe Komuesa, the President of the Community of Mennonite Churches in Congo (CMCO), talked at length about how Lodema made all the difference in his life. As a student, there came a time when he had to face the school leaders for an oral exam to see if he would be approved to advance to the next level of academic standing. Knowing that she would be part of the panel made him work that much harder to be certain he would be prepared for the questions and challenges of the testing. He still uses much of that experience when he works with new pastors or in his own teaching because he knows how effective Lodema's strong discipline and high expectations was for him.

Maybe someday, the dreams of Independence will come true for every citizen of Congo. One thing for sure though, the dreams have changed from not having to work or study to a dream to just be able to work at a good job and study in a quality school. This truth was confirmed in 2012, when one of Lodema's students, who graduated in 1965 from Miodi Lycee *walked* over twenty miles (one way) to greet this author and deliver that very message.

Julie Katambue was the first and only woman from her family to attend advanced schooling opportunities and it has made all the difference in her life. This is one more example to those who will listen that if you want to change the world, then change it one child; one student; and one family at a time by feeding their soul and their mind with the truth of the Gospel. This is what the missionaries of Congo and Nyanga were dedicated to doing. This is why they felt they were *home* when they could serve by teaching, healing, preaching, and preparing those who lived in Congo for living for Christ.

Julie shares her pictures of Lodema and her graduation certificate along with the program from the graduation ceremonies to the author. (Picture provided by author, July, 2012)

Do you have that question in your mind about whether or not you are *home* right now? Imagine being chased out of a country that was under siege. And then imagine that when most people would think that they are finally *safe* by being out of harm's way, there is emptiness and a feeling of dislocation because a higher power is calling you back to that very place. Deep down this is where Lodema was during this period from the 1960 Evacuation until she returned and landed in Nyanga in August of 1962. Where is home? Where is home indeed? It is only where God calls us!

If God is calling you to another place it is time to pursue that calling! Your experience will not be like Lodema's nor will it be guaranteed to be any safer or less dangerous. This may be a good time to stop reading this book and read Luke chapters nine and ten about coming home. Reminding each of us about who God wants us to regard as our neighbor will also allow us to better understand where our home is.

Julie's diploma and the program from her graduation ceremony that took place in June, 1965, were important enough to her to bring them with her on a forty mile walk to be interviewed. Her educational and academic experiences of having a teacher like Lodema have never been lost on her life or any of those whom she has touched and influenced. Wouldn't we all like to leave such a legacy?

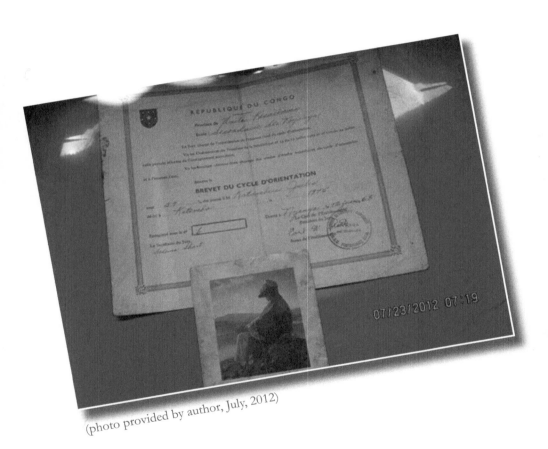

(photo provided by author, July, 2012)

How Did We Get Here?

"Therefore, my brothers, be all the more eager to make your calling and election sure. For if you do these things, you will never fall, and you will receive a rich welcome into the eternal kingdom of our Lord and Savior Jesus Christ." II Peter 1:10-11 (NIV)

Lodema was born into a farm family near Archbold, Ohio, on February 16, 1916. Her two older brothers, Fred and Laurel, could not have been more different. It seems you could also say the same about her younger sister Isabelle. Her father Albert P. Short was adept at acquiring things, and his ability to purchase farms and operate as a small business man doing carpentry and construction projects around the farm helped to pay the bills as well as the farms themselves.

Her mother Elizabeth was a school teacher, and she set a solid pattern early on for both girls to get an education and a teaching certificate to be self-sufficient. Both parents seemed like they had been prepared to meet the coming economic challenges of the Great Depression. It was during the height of this economic downturn that Lodema grew up and became a teenager, college student, and a school teacher just like her Mom.

Lodema attended high school in a small village near their farm called Ridgeville Corners. This was a very small community and the *corners* were important because a significant highway, US Route 6, went through the middle of town. It was crisscrossed by what most people thought was an old Indian trail used by Native Americans who traversed that part of the world, trading furs and other items in the early nineteenth century. The few businesses in town were a grocery general store, a blacksmith and general fixit shop, and of course the school.

Tennis was big then, and they even had a women's basketball team that was very competitive. The entire basketball schedule might include four games against local competition, but even that was quite progressive at that time. Lodema's future sister-in-law, Ada Arnos Arps, was her classmate at Ridgeville Corners and also attended Bowling Green Normal at the same time.

Lodema's parents were insistent on her and Isabelle both getting college training after high school, and both girls went to Bowling Green Normal School (now known as Bowling Green State University) and got their teaching certificates. To say this was progressive thinking on the part of her parents would grossly understate its importance in her future career. Young girls were not encouraged to leave home for college life when this was normally the realm of the young men of the families in the 1920's and 30's.

While the rest of America was going through The Depression, the members of the Albert P. Short house were too busy working to notice how difficult the world around them really was. Hard work became the theme by which all problems could be solved, and if you raised your head long enough to think about it, a swift kick in the pants would help you refocus. It seemed that mother Elizabeth was one of the better kickers in those days. She left no question in her children's minds about the importance of hard work, whether it was in the classroom or in weeding the garden.

The Short family also used reverse psychology on their sons. It may have been popular to send the sons to college and domesticate the daughters, but Albert and Elizabeth Short decided that their boys should stay home and become farmers while the girls went off to college to prepare for teaching. That was fine with Lodema's brother Fred who took to farming just fine, and school was never that much fun. Laurel, on the other hand, didn't like school much either, but he also didn't like the smell of the cows and pigs. Laurel would choose to help his Dad cut wood and learn carpentry whenever given the chance, and this became more of his responsibility. This turned out just fine with him when Albert decided they could make money on the side working as carpenters and hiring out when neighbors were building houses and barns. Fred never quite saw all of that as the best master plan, but when he ended up with one of the farms as a reward for all of his years of work; it probably all evened out.

While the secular and educational part of Lodema's life was going along, there was also the part of the family life that was built around the importance of church. They never missed a Sunday or midweek service at the Archbold Defenseless Mennonite Church, and they always dressed in Sunday clothes. These clothes were different and special, and it always included a Saturday night bath, which was needed on the farm. The bath part might have been moved up to Friday on some weeks when a family gathering would take place. Albert read the Bible around the kitchen table to the kids, and there was little goofing around if you remember the thing about the kicks in the pants. Lodema seemed to respond to the Word of God more than the other children.

We don't know why, but Lodema's deep faith was to be seen later on when we she chose to attend Moody Bible Institute for training to become a missionary. This took place for the most part in the Mennonite church in Archbold. Pastor Earl Slagle could pierce even the faintest heart as he would challenge his listeners with the truth of the Gospel of Jesus Christ. The successor Pastor at the Archbold Evangelical Mennonite Church (EMC), Harry Bertsche, would also have a big impact on Lodema's life. She loved hearing his sermons when she came home from Congo, but most of all she became lifelong friends with Harry's son, Jim Bertsche, and his family who became colleagues in the Congo.

Lodema grew in her faith during the time she was a young school teacher in the Archbold area. She participated in church activities including youth group and women's group's events. When missionaries came to town to share their calling, she listened intently to their stories. Then one day, Archie Graber returned from a place called Congo and shared how he was called to help build churches, schools, and homes for missionaries so that they could share the Gospel, but also provide a leg up to those who have great needs. Archie was from nearby Stryker, Ohio, and his message was that you don't have to do something different to be a missionary, but you can take the talents and skills that God has given you and give them back in a different way in a different place. Most important he said, "Make sure God is calling you to go!"

Lodema was an important part of the family when it came to being the peacemaker. After returning from college in the mid 1930's, she was an important asset to the family in supporting her parents as well as being a good diplomat with her brothers. When her younger sister Isabelle became anxious to leave the farm and move on to other things like marriage and moving to the city, Lodema patched things up with Mom and Dad. She and Isabelle both started teaching at local one room schools near the family farm.

Lodema's first teaching assignment was at the Spiess School just south of Archbold. It was 1937, and her Brother Laurel's oldest child, Laurel, Jr., was just starting school and was to be one of her students. She thought all summer about how this dynamic might work out since she didn't want the parents of the other children to think she would favor him in any way for special treatment.

Lodema's nephew/student Laurel J became a real project when school started that fall. He could not speak English because German had been the family language at home, and the lessons seemed like a mystery story with no translators. Lodema was adamant that she would not cut her nephew any slack, and Laurel J thought all of this was too much to expect from a little six year old kid. He rebelled!

Lodema would have none of it, even if he was her brother's son! As fall moved to winter, the crustiness of teacher and student deepened. John Lohse, one of the older students, remembers that Lodema was the most incredible teacher that he ever had. But he also remembered how Laurel J did not share this same sentiment at that time. This was one of the worst winters on record for cold, ice, and snow, and on several days the school had to be closed for weather conditions.

Even when the school was open, the kids would go out to play and get wet from the snow ball fights and rolling in the snow. The worst day of that winter was when several of the parents got stuck trying to drive their kids to school. John also was one of the kids who got soaked on a cold wintry day and when he returned to the classroom, Lodema pulled off most of his clothes and placed them on the wood burning stove to dry while he sat in a blanket next to it. Even then, he could sense through her frustration with him that she just had his best interests at heart. He never forgot her sense of caring and nurturing for her students.

Laurel J's rebellion and frustration reached its peak soon after the winter freeze and during the spring thaw. He was doing better in school by now, but it still seemed that Lodema was going out of her way to expect more from him than she did from the others. He was correct in thinking this because this is how Albert P. and Elizabeth had raised her. You get what you expect in life, and if you don't start with high expectations you won't see high achievement. But Laurel J decided one day to fight back against what he thought was the tyranny of his plight as nephew of the teacher.

All the kids had returned to the school room and he was the last one in from the playground. As an older kid slammed the door on him he realized that he could play a trick on everyone by closing the latch on the door and sliding a piece of wood into it to cinch it so tight, no one could open it. Now he had everyone locked in the school and he was the only one on the playground! Let's see how that plays out! It didn't go as well as he thought.

Eventually, Donald Buerher slid out the window after teacher Lodema had instructed her nephew to remove the inventive wooden lock and Don was able to remove it. From that point forward, the punishment and anguish of the moment were opportunities to build a new relationship between teacher-student and aunt-nephew.

At the end of that year, Laurel J was able to fill in for an older student in a play that was being performed for the parents. Not only did he play a role far beyond his years, he brought the house down with laughter on several lines, which he remembered for many years to come. Who knows the importance of lessons learned that year, the first year teacher who was to become a *teacher of teachers* in the Congo, or Laurel J, the future entrepreneur and ham radio operator who would give witness to many souls in China? Here is Laurel's recollection of a play in which he stepped in at the last minute to help Lodema when an older boy got sick and could not perform in the play:

"...the play was basically for the seventh and eighth graders. As a first grader I was not considered for the play. The play was a Hero-Villain variety which was popular at that time. It is correct that the boy playing the villain became ill the day before the presentation. In a one room school recitals for eight grades all take place in the front of the school. The play rehearsal also took place in the front. Since I had heard the lines numerous time I had memorized and showed Lodema that fact, and she quickly put me in the play as the villain.

The play was a big hit if you can imagine a six-year old boy with a handlebar mustache reciting lines, and since my English was still limited the meaning of many of the words were unknown to me. There were many laughs by the audience and the play was a big hit. I think this helped to alleviate some of my previous bad behavior..."

Lodema's teaching career then sent her to the village schools in Archbold after two years in German Township's Spiess School. But, she would remember the lessons of Spiess School for all of her life as did her students. Treating all her students with dignity, respect, and high expectations would help her in times of working with students at all levels.

Lodema never missed the opportunity to hear stories of missionaries. When she heard about the progress being made by Archie Graber and the people who were in Kalonda, she kept thinking that maybe God might have a place for her in Congo. She had saved enough money from eight years of teaching that in 1943 she left for Chicago to attend Moody Bible Institute. There was a track specifically set up to help channel missionaries into the places in the world that were open to the Gospel. Many of her friends decided to take Spanish since so many people were being called to serve in Central and South America. But somehow, Lodema felt God's call on her life to learn French. It was one more little decision that turned out to have huge consequences as the French students were being prepared for Africa.

She completed her work at Moody and kept in close contact with the Grabers about the possibilities in Congo. They were very encouraging as they had just completed two more school buildings in the Tshikapa area, and the need for teachers had never been greater. Could it be that she would one day be using her teaching skills in Congo? That did seem like a long way from **HOME!**

By 1947, Lodema was on her way to Congo for her first term as a missionary. She made a significant first stop in Brussels, Belgium, to be the first CIM Missionary to complete the Belgium Colonial Course. Her first stop in the Belgian Congo was in Mutena. She stayed in a house with three other women whose last names all began with the initial "S." The friendship of the three "S's" would build many lifetime memories between them. The other women whose last name began with "S" were Mabel Sauder, Lois Slagle, and Fanny Schmallenberger, and they were part of that group (see Chapter 1) who went to Lake Madimape before evacuating in 1960. They also would return as Lodema did to Congo to fulfill their calling just a few years later. Teaching school would never be ordinary again! It was a calling!

It was an honor for Lodema to become known as Momma Kane-mu (Ka-nay-mu). We believe this name, which means honor, integrity, respect, and trustworthiness, was conveyed by the church council at Mutena that was made up of the local Congolese leaders. Jim Bertsche was an admirer of Lodema's, and although he could not confirm the actual source of the conveyance of *Kanemu*, he thought the meaning to be more like, *"has to do with pleasantness, helpfulness, gentleness."*

The uniqueness of names such as this in Congo is quite important. Unlike America, where anyone can call themselves anything they want and then publicize it, in Congo, only the people can grant you the honor of such a name. When she was transferred to the new school being built in Nyanga, the name stuck for the next thirty-four years. Knowing that you have a name given to you by those you serve is unique and special! Maybe that's why she thought of Congo as **HOME!**

The Nyanga mission station staff picture from the early 1950's. Lodema is the second from right in the front row. Frank and Agnes Entz, 2nd & 3rd left in back row. Sam and Leona Entz are back and front on the right side Congolese Pastor Ngongo David is front left. (Picture is provided by Wanda Short, niece of Lodema)

Lodema's first class at Spiess School, circa 1935-36, last row L to R, Martie Lugbill, Mary Eicher, Bernice Beck, Charles Winzeler. Second from rear: L to R. Robert Lohse, (John›s older brother) James Eicher, Donna Lugbill, Herbert Buerher, Donald Buerher. Third from rear, L to R John Lohse, Bernice Roth. Front Row, L to R Walter Lohse, (fellow first grader) Phyllis Roth, Laurel J. Short (author's first cousin). (Photo provided by John Lohse and confirmed by Laurel J. Short)

"C.I.M.'s Happy Singers"

Front, left to right; Kakesa Leonard, Mukedi; Mbuya Zachee, Nyanga; Mukanzu Louis, Nyanga; Ngandu Leon, Charlesville.
Bar. left to right; Kidinda David, Mukedi; Ilunga Maurice, Charlesville; Tshiloba Edouard, Charlesville; Mpoi George, Tshikapa; Mbualungu Theodore, Mukedi.

Nine Happy Singers

"These things I have spoken to you, that my joy may be in you, and that your joy may be full." John 15:11 (RSV)

In the late 1950's, European colonization in Africa was reaching a conclusion. The Europeans didn't fully realize it, and for sure they didn't think it would happen quite the way it turned out. Belgium was not alone in this public relations quandary, but every chance they got to show the world how valuable their presence had been in the Congo, they liked to take advantage of it. So when the Belgian school inspector told the missionaries of the Congo Inland Mission in Tshikapa that they would like some positive examples of *civilized Africans* (the Belgian official's distinction) who could perform at the Brussels World's Fair, many thought that would be a great day for their Congolese students.

The *Nine Happy Singers* from the Congo shattered more stereotypes in that visit than either the Belgians or the missionaries could have imagined. Their names and their home villages from 1958 are:

- Leonard Kakesa, from Mukedi
- Zachee Mbuya, from Nyanga
- Louis Mukanzu, from Nyanga
- Leon Ngandu, from Charlesville
- David Kidinda, from Mukedi
- Maurice Ilunga, from Charlesville
- Edouard Tshiloba, from Charlesville
- George Mpoi, from Tshikapa
- Theodore Mbualungu, from Mukedi

These men had never traveled more than one hundred miles from their place of birth, and there was some concern about cultural issues to say the least. How would they relate to large crowds at a venue of this magnitude? How would they relate to an area of the world that to that point had very few black residents, as the men would discover when they arrived in Brussels?

Some people actually came up to them and wanted to touch them and see if their skin was real or if the pigment of their skin might actually rub off. This was not shocking to those who lived in Europe at that time since other World's Fairs had been held in previous years and the exhibits that included citizens from colonized nations often treated them as primitive animals.

It didn't take long for the stories to start circulating that these men were indeed different. They could sing in multiple languages, but especially in French with vivid four part harmony. They could answer questions about their homeland in articulate ways that would seem normal to most readers today, but in 1958, this was not expected. Many people were still thinking that audible grunts and arm motions were the most that could be expected of them.

The Belgian authorities had intentionally built an African complex at Turveren, home of the Central Africa Museum, so they would have a comfortable place to stay. That is political speak for, *let's keep them off the streets and out of the hotels in Brussels*, and thus you had their form of segregation from civilized folks.

This did not work so well since Lodema had spent time in Brussels in 1947 when she was the first CIM Missionary to take the Belgian Colonial Course, and while there, she got to know many families in the Mennonite and Anabaptist Churches. The Congo *Happy Singers* suddenly were a hot topic and Belgians came in car caravans to take them to local churches and homes in their city. Lodema warned them to be on their best behavior at all times since they were representing not just their families and the school at Nyanga, but indeed their entire country of Congo and without actually saying it… the entire Negro race.

Lodema was not naïve about the racist issues that surrounded these events. She had seen maturity even among the missionaries on this issue of subservience. In her heart she often subdued her feelings about racist colonial issues because, like the other missionaries, she had to abide by the existing rules of the state. Knowing from afar that corruption and greed were the primary motivations for many colonial authorities did not change her calling or her message. Sharing the Gospel came first, teaching usable skills came second, and helping make sociological strides came whenever possible. Brussels in 1958 allowed the possibility of sociological impact. She would not miss that chance for these men.

Maurice, Theodore, and Leonard quickly became popular soloists when they visited churches and private homes. The entire nine members could harmonize on the run without music even though they could all read music to a small extent. One of the favorites of audiences was the song, *His Eye Is On the Sparrow* and when the lyrics said, "...but I know He watches me!" there were many tears of joy shed. This joy personified the fact that people were discovering new brothers and sisters in the Lord. There was also joy inside the hearts of these young men because they too understood in part the significance of their success.

They had never seen homes as large as the ones they were visiting. Indoor plumbing was a new and novel idea that started to make more sense the longer they spent time in Brussels. Thankfully, the training that Allan Wiebe, Art Janz, and of course Lodema was paying off big time. Personal grooming and deodorant were not the same as in Congo and the dress codes were indeed hard to get used to. One thing about these men though, you could dress them up in their powder blue suits and everyone was proud to ask them out and be part of their homes and churches. That's not to say they were not just as much fun and just as likely to fit in when they dressed down in more casual attire as well.

One of the young men, Nganda Leon, was a couple of years older than the other members of the choir. He had lobbied Lodema for years to have separate choirs for those who could sing better and had an interest in music from those who found themselves in choir because it was required. The work and effort in training this group was evidence for his case that an elite group of gifted singers could achieve much greater competency and a greater sense of reward for their efforts. Lodema reluctantly had to agree with him. The nine *Happy Singers* became a focal point for great achievement as well as opening new doors and ideas for the singers themselves.

Several of these men would continue their education toward college degrees, and some would study in the USA and attend universities there. All of them would agree to this day, that the experience they had in Belgium in 1958, would change their lives forever. In order to bring some perspective to this event and its meaning, we cannot avoid an open discussion of racism and how it was perceived both then and in the years following both the World's Fair in 1958, and Independence in 1960.

The bloody events that took place in 1960 were an overt attempt to break away from the very same country that had hosted this World's Fair just two years earlier. The behavior and the policies of the Belgian Leaders were naïve to say the least. For many years they attempted to re-write history to deflect any blame or responsibility for the legacy they and their Western allies such as the USA and Britain had left behind.

Just before one of the singing performances at the World's Fair, there was an interesting greeting that took place that might have caused an uproar. As the men from Congo were finishing their performance, three screaming children ran up on the stage and ran toward them. The screams were expressions of joy as the three children of Jim and Jenny Bertsche could not contain their happiness to see their friends from Congo. Sandra, Linda, and Tim were so happy to see these familiar faces from their mission home in Congo that they charged forward and grabbed the men by their legs and hugged them like long lost family members.

This spontaneous show of love and respect was not that surprising to Jim and Jenny, but the people surrounding the exhibit did not know what to say or how to deal with white children, embracing these young black men. Remember the Belgians had intentionally built the tents in the compound at the Central Africa Museum at Terveren so that they would not have this kind of dilemma. It was not a problem, the men knelt down and gave each child a hug and thanked them for coming to their show just like it would have been back in Nyanga. The children returned to their parents happy to have heard them sing as were all the others in attendance. They were all impressed by the competence and maturity of the Congolese *Happy Singers*.

The Bertsche's were actually on their way home to the USA and planned their trip to go through Brussels for the chance to see the singers during the World's Fair. They did not plan to be part of a sociological experiment, nor did they think of their children as being endangered by having contact with Africans. In fact, this same calling they felt as young servants of God, being called by Christ to serve in Africa, was indeed the joy of their life.

This small snippet of time in Brussels in 1958 helped them realize their lives were not just confined to small villages in

Happy Singers visiting Belgians outside the World's Fair in Brussels, 1958 (pictures provided by Maurice Ilunga, Kinshasa 2012.)

Congo, but indeed would have worldwide implications as their students and colleagues from the Congo would play roles on many stages throughout the world. Their children adopted a similar world view and also responded to God's calling in each of their lives by serving in various parts of Congo and Africa.

The *Happy Singers* performed three times a day, four days a week in two separate locations at the Fair. In addition to performing at several local churches, they visited many Belgian homes and spent time almost everywhere except at Terverun. News of their popularity would prompt many others to invite the men to events and venues that were unscheduled and random. No doubt this bothered many of the Belgian officials, but not to the point of trying to intervene or alter these meetings.

What started out to be a novelty for some of the Belgians who invited the singers into their homes and churches, turned into an important lesson in understanding the huge upside potential of the people who occupied their colony in Africa. No longer would they regard inhabitants of the Congo as submissive, indolent, dangerous, or ignorant brothers.

At the time of the writing of this book, there are four living survivors from the choir. All four of them, Theodore Mbualungu, Maurice Ilunga, Zachee Mbuya, and Leon Ngandu were interviewed about this experience in July of 2012. They were very open in their responses to a variety of questions about their time in Brussels in 1958, and also their relationship with Lodema and the missionaries in general. They were uniform in their appreciation of what all the mission schools and churches had done for them and their families. They also talked about their unique experience in how their lives had been formed and influenced by these same individuals and institutions.

When asked about their recollections of Lodema, they were all uniform in responding that she brought unusual discipline to the class room and thereby to their lives as they sought to emulate that in their own work. They were also quick to point out that as they grew older they remembered the level of respect all the missionaries had shown to them. This became an important lesson as they would travel to other parts of the country and even to other parts of the world. The role that racism would play in the way people treated others, was never lost on the example that Lodema and her colleagues of the CIM/AIMM brought to the table in a positive way.

One of the questions that I posed to them centered on the idea of how they would have advised missionaries like Lodema after the 1960 Independence Evacuation. Knowing what they experienced living in Congo, what advice would they have given to someone like Lodema if that were their sister, or mother? Would they have advised them to return to Congo?

The room went silent for a few seconds… "I would have told her NOT to come back" said Maurice.

Theodore and Leon agreed. "We are glad that they did return as soon as they did because we needed them for sure!"

Zachee indicated in a separate interview that he too would not have advised a family member to return as they did in 1962 as there was severe violence and political turmoil in many of the villages.

Their reflections were evidence enough that Lodema's bravery, adherence to her calling, and her desire to serve in Congo could only have come from God. Mortal men would not sign up for this duty. Only those who know where **Home** is!

Several of the choir members, along with other outstanding students, were chosen after the World's Fair to come to the USA to at-

Picture from left to right: Theodore Mbualungu; D Short, author; Maurice Ilunga (photo from author DL Short, July, 2012)

tend college. They struggled with the formal English language for a time, but eventually did very well, and almost all graduated with both undergraduate and graduate degrees. Even today, there are professors, pastors, teachers, entrepreneurs, doctors, nurses, attorneys, and professionals of all types who have been the beneficiary of these schools that were started by Lodema and her colleagues.

This watershed event from the World's Fair can never be underestimated. The men came home to great adulation. Other students could hardly wait to hear about their trip and to change their dreams based on what the *Happy Singers* had experienced. Understanding that people are capable of achieving at high levels has been suppressed for so long in the counties of Africa that it will take many generations to reverse that belief. What these men did with their lives, not only in 1958 but in the years to follow, is a microcosm of the potential we have lost from that suppression. We know there are many more capable students just like them!

Even in his seventies and with some significant health problems, Theodore has begun a new church in Kinshasa and continues to serve

From left to right: Theodore Mbualungu; the author D Short; Maurice Ilungu; Leon Ngandu (photo by author, DL Short, July 2012)

the Lord. Maurice (in Kinshasa) is not quite as active but still attends church faithfully and remembers how to carry his part of the harmony when hymns are being sung. Zachee (living in Nyanga) and Leon (in Kinshasa) are still living vital lives of service and know that their impact on providing a path for others to move into professional careers as teachers, pastors, and leaders has never been forgotten.

When the nine *Happy Singers* set this pattern of excellence for the entire world to see, they also set a witness for the students coming behind them to look higher and believe achievement would be possible for them as well. Lodema and all of the missionaries from this era would be so happy to know this legacy! They not only heard the Gospel, they lived out the Gospel in both actions and example.

Oh No! You are Not Going Back to Congo!

"Through him we have obtained access to this grace in which we stand, and we rejoice in our hope of sharing the glory of God. More than that, we rejoice in our sufferings, knowing that suffering produces endurance, and endurance produces character, and character produces hope..." Romans 5:2-4 (RSV)

Those words kept resonating from Lodema's family members and even some of her friends. Most of them were not so direct or brazen in this almost command type statement. But, make no mistake about it; they did not favor her going back to a country whose violence was still increasing. Couple that with the fact that she had to be life-flighted out of the country by United Nations relief planes and the obvious fact that there were many other places in the world that needed a teacher who could also share the Gospel.

As we discovered in the last chapter, even the surviving Congolese *Happy Singers* would have given this same advice if they were pressed by family members about returning to Congo in 1962. There were horrific examples of more than a million people who had been run out of their homes and pushed into refugee camps since the missionaries had left in 1960. Some families had to hide in the bush country with forested protection from those who had taken over their homes. Why indeed go back, and of all things, why go back now?

Archie Graber, whose influence was most vital in Lodema's early calling, had been one of the missionaries from the CIM who returned to what was now being called Zaire (pronounced Zi ear) in late 1960 and early 1961. There were starving people and no way to get food and supplies to them in the southern provinces of Zaire. Political forces were more volatile than ever and the current leader of the country, Patrice Lumumba, was a flash point for this volatility. As we pointed out in earlier segments of this book, Lumumba would be assassinated with the help of the CIA and the opportunistic Mr. Mbutu.

The story of how Archie was able to help the UN deliver food and supplies to starving masses was best told in a book by Levi Keidel called, *War To Be One*. For our story, we will skip some of the details of that most important endeavor, but a few of the details are important to set the stage for understanding why this was determined to be a good time to have more missionaries return to Congo. We ask the reader's indulgence also in that we will continue to refer to the country as Congo. Just for the record, here is a listing of how the country's name has evolved over time:

- Congo Free State 1877 to 1908
- Belgian Congo 1908 to 1960
- Republic of Congo (period for the first ten years after Independence) 1960-71
- Zaire 1971- 1997
- Democratic Republic of Congo (DRC) 1998 to present

Meanwhile, Lodema's life had taken some unusual turns while she was home on that unscheduled two year furlough. Her oldest brother Fred died suddenly from a pulmonary embolism following surgery in January, 1961. Fred's wife Jeanette had always been one of Lodema's most loyal supporters, and now she was able to offer prayer support and encouragement to Fred's family. This would not have happened of course if she were in the Congo. This also was an opportunity to bring some unity to her sister Isabelle and her surviving brother Laurel. Laurel also lived in Archbold, and was a big help to Lodema in taking care of her home and helping her with mundane projects like buying a car and keeping up on taxes, etc.

Speaking of cars, the Rich Brothers Ford dealership in Archbold, Ohio was always there for Lodema to help her with a car when she returned for her furloughs. Little did she know that in addition to providing steady wheels for her transportation needs, one of the sons of that dealership, namely Philip Rich and his wife, would become missionaries one day and serve with Lodema in Congo. Yes, there is hope for used car salesmen and stock brokers as well!

The other aspect of Lodema's life had to do with getting comfortable back at **HOME** in the USA. Church life and being around family became much easier than ever, and the thought of never going back to Congo was now being balanced by a life that was beginning to feel pretty good. She was also able to complete her Bachelor of Science and Masters in Education degree at Bowling Green, and that would open up more teaching opportunities than ever.

There was quite a difference in the campus at BGSU from 1934 when she last was there, but she handled being a student almost as well as she handled being a teacher. She was just about to take on a full time teaching position in Wauseon, Ohio, when the call came from Harve Driver. Archie Graber had just returned from Congo, and he believed the time was right for the teachers to return to Nyanga to re-ignite the work there.

They needed experienced people who could handle the difficult challenges that would be part of such a return. When Lodema arrived home from the Congo in 1960, she would have jumped for joy to turn around and return immediately. Now she needed to pray and reflect again on whether all of these positive experiences she had since coming back home were a message that she should stay in the USA? Her quandary was quickly answered by her favorite Bible passage: I Thessalonians 5:23-24 (Revised Standard Version) *"May the God of peace himself sanctify you wholly; and may your spirit and soul and body be kept sound and blameless at the coming of our Lord Jesus Christ. He who calls you is faithful and he will do it."*

She prayed for guidance and sought the Lord about whether she should return to Congo. Just as she was convinced of her calling in the 1940's when she was at The Moody Bible Institute, she was equally convinced that this was where she should return **HOME** once again. The encouragement she experienced in the two years back in Ohio would never return void as the people she touched in the Evangelical Mennonite Churches would become her biggest supporters and prayer partners. Yes, even her family understood grudgingly that this diminutive woman in her mid-forties was determined to fulfill and return to her calling.

Instead of "NO, NO please don't go," the nieces, nephews, and family members tried to surround her with encouragement to follow her dreams and calling. You can see the differences in maturity by the

To Congo —
To teach that they may " . . . be able to teach others also."

Lodema E. Short
B. P. 1 Tshikapa
Republic of Congo (Kinshasa)

O teach me, Lord, that I may teach
The precious things
Thou dost impart;
And wing my words,
that they may reach,
The hidden depths of many a heart.

Frances R. Havergal

Home address:
CONGO INLAND MISSION
251 W. Hively Avenue
Elkhart, Indiana 46514

prayer cards shown below as the young woman becomes the mature missionary woman better known as Momma Kanemu. She loved that name every bit as much as Lodema.

When the missionaries arrived back on the field in the post-Independence period there were some significant changes. The leaders of the churches and the denomination within Congo had always been the missionary leaders. The pastors would serve at the behest of the missionary leaders, and there was no hierarchy that provided for the Con-

This picture includes former students. Left to right: your author; Zachee Mbuyi, member of the 1958 *Happy Singers* who performed at the Brussels World's Fair; current headmistress at Miodi Tech, Madame Bernadette Manya; Pastor Komesa, Head of the Mennonite Church of Congo and a resident of Nyanga and former student of Lodema's; two pastors from Nyanga who had Lodema as a teacher.

golese pastors to provide leadership except to other Congolese within their churches. Did *Independence* have to take place inside the church as well as outside? Was this really a good idea when we don't know how things will play out?

Miodi Technical School as it stands today in Nyanga (picture by author DL Short)

Classrooms at the Miodi Technical School in Nyanga where Lodema taught and as
they are still in use today to train both men and women for all types of professional
roles in Congo. (Photo by author DL Short, July 2012)

The people of Congo Inland Mission were confronted with the reality that what is good for the goose would have to be good for the gander. From 1962 to 1985, there was an almost complete surrender of the control of the churches to the Congolese pastors and church leaders. Many aspects of the schools were to move in the same direction. Consequently, the school that Lodema returned to would eventually do more than train students to move into society. It also became a teacher training institute that would perpetuate the educational progress that had been established. There was also great foresight in adding a girl's school to the curriculum so that teachers and nurses and professionals could be developed from the female population of Congo as well as the males.

The greatest testament to these changes is that many of these same schools are still surviving today, and serving to help people just as they were designed to do back in the 1960's. The Miodi School of that era is now called Miodi Tech, and averages two hundred students enrolled each year. Some of Lodema's students serve as teachers, pastors, and community leaders to perpetuate this dream and calling. The dream is that, given a chance at learning in a safe and qualified school, African children are capable and blessed with the ability to learn, grow, and become contributing members of society.

The sleepy village of Nyanga looks a lot like it did in 1965. The school buildings are weathered for sure, but they still house students and classrooms where kids study and grow up. Had Lodema and her colleagues not returned to Congo when they did, there is a high likelihood there would be ten thousand fewer kids who received an education and a leg up in life. They can all be blessed by the fact that Lodema felt like this was **HOME**!

Training Teachers Will Make a Difference

And his gifts were that some should be apostles, some prophets, some evangelists, some pastors and <u>teachers</u>, for the equipment of the saints, for the work of ministry, for building up the body of Christ..." Ephesians 4:11-12 (RSV)

During the colonial period from 1908 to 1960, missionaries had been the most reliable source of manpower to fill jobs that were not filled from secular and traditional sources. One of the greatest gaps in the broad picture of independent Zaire of 1960 and beyond, compared to the colonial period of the Belgian Congo, was the number of competent and trained personnel required to fill so many positions in the government, hospitals, and schools. Abruptly after Independence, the Catholic and Protestant mission schools were staffed by Congolese. In the outlying villages like Nyanga, that was not an easy task as new teachers were not trained or ready for such responsibility.

Will he hear?

Lodema became inspired to paint, and she loved the arts. She was ultimately successful in transferring some of her passion to many students in Congo. Once, when she was just starting to express herself on canvas during her first furlough in 1952, one of her nephews was watching intently as she was stroking oil paints to a burlap canvas. She was re-creating a scene from her home in Congo, and the African boy that was in the picture was a reminder of her students. The young man was sitting at an angle and only one ear was showing so her young nephew asked her the question, "Will he be able to hear?"

She stopped what she was doing because she had been deep in thought about her return to Africa in a few months and asked again why her nephew was concerned about him hearing. She thought perhaps he was concerned that the African boy would be able to *hear the Gospel,* but in fact her nephew was thinking the boy in the picture only had one ear and perhaps was deaf.

Lodema's thinking during her entire time in Congo was that strong academic and formal schooling would be the most empowering gift she could give to those who were in her classes. Indeed, she wanted all of them *to hear.*

She loved the idea so much that she entitled the picture "Will he hear?" This was the passion of Lodema and all of her colleagues for the kids they taught, the adults they counseled, and the entire community that they ministered to in the churches, hospitals, schools, and farms where they worked to improve learning and productivity. The same question is being asked

even now by all who have a heart for the people of Congo. Will they hear? Year after year, classes of graduates such as the one below with Lodema and Fanny Schmallenberger entered the work place and advanced professional schools because of their work.

Most of the schools and infrastructure in Congo are worse off today than they were in 1960 when Independence took place. Not enough teachers, doctors, nurses, and professionals in every walk of life have been produced from the educational system. The nation's abundant natural resources are the envy of the world, but their translation to help the average Congolese Citizen is sadly missing as one can see in the conditions of the schools, roads, and general infrastructure.

If the secular government of Congo had only followed the discipline and planning that the CIM Missionaries had developed, the country would be a much different place. Making sure that the first fruits of the mining industry remained in the country for the citizens of Congo would have made all the difference. In fact, it would still make a huge difference even today if the graft and corruption ended.

Prior to Independence, the Belgian Colonial Government operated at the behest and priorities of the Belgian government and their western allies. The uranium used to build the atomic bombs for the Second World War came from the Congo. Strategic minerals such as cobalt and later industrial diamonds along with gold and many others all kept flowing out of the country to the benefit of countless corporations, governments, and individuals, but not so much to the people of Congo.

What does all of this have to do with teacher training? During this time, the infrastructure that was being built was mostly being done through the efforts of missionary groups. The Belgian subsidies were real, but they were also a quid pro quo for expected allegiance to the colonial authorities.

Let me give you a real world example of how this equation was working. The Belgian government believed that teaching Christianity in their Congo Colony was the moral thing to do. As a predominately Catholic nation, Belgium authorized subsidizing the Catholic mission stations and personnel at almost 100% of their salaries to encourage their establishment. This strategy began in the period just after Belgium fired their Royal Leader, King Leopold II, and took over the Congo colony themselves in 1908. The opening for other denominations to send missionaries began almost immediately thereafter with many of the Protestant missionaries being relegated to more of the rural outlying areas in what is often referred to as the bush country.

This arrangement was the lowest cost way for Belgium to appear to be doing admirable work among the people of Congo, when in fact they were getting the churches and mission organizations to build much of their infrastructure such as schools and hospitals for a fraction of what it would have cost them to do it with traditionally secular resources and people. They referred to Catholic Missionaries as *Domestic* missionaries, while Protestants were known as *Foreign* missionaries. Protestant missions were then for the most part being financed by the denominations and local churches from their place of origin.

The mission fields of Congo, it turns out, were *white unto harvest* and the success of these mission agencies was in fact one of the greatest successes, but least told stories about Congo. The term *white unto harvest* is a Biblical term that indicates that people were ready to hear the Gospel and respond to it in positive ways. This success came at a dangerous price to Belgium. All of these Protestant mission groups were having significant influence among the people, and this was starting to be a threat to the colonial powers.

The politicos in Brussels tried to reign in the Protestants to have as much loyalty as their Catholic brethren. Starting just after the end of World War II, they began to offer what was known as the *colonial course* for foreign missionaries to be taken for three months in Belgium. Lodema Short was chosen to be the first CIM missionary to take the course in 1947. Once the course was completed, her salary would be re-imbursed at 85% of the annual total by Belgium. This money was greatly appreciated, even if it came at the expense of having to interpret colonial propaganda and revisionist history.

In fact, every Protestant Missionary who took the course would receive the same stipend so the incentive was high for all of the CIM missionaries to spend time in Belgium as soon as possible, or before they took their first assignment in Congo, to complete this course. It is hard to figure why it took three months to teach intelligent missionaries that Belgium was the best thing that had ever happened to the Congo. Convincing those who were called in the name of Jesus Christ that their allegiance to the Belgian government should be just barely a notch below that divine level required some fancy French phraseology. Of course, the check for eight-five percent of their annual salary each year was also intended to impact that allegiance.

Government propaganda it turns out was not limited to the general populace of Belgium when describing Belgium's role in Congo. The whole world, along with the Belgian citizens, was fed a flurry of revisionist history that portrayed King Leopold II to be a humanitarian. Much of this same story was capsulized and then taught to the missionaries who ended up taking the *colonial course.*

It is easier to reflect on many of these issues with the luxury of 20/20 hindsight. Seeing this course for what it was long after the end of colonial rule was hardly so clear in 1947 when Lodema was paving the way for others to take the same course. It was deemed to be a requirement to be able to do ministry in Congo. There was no such thing as the book by Adam Hochschild called *King Leopold's Ghost (*1998) to examine the track record of the King that appeared in this course to be more hero and visionary than villain and thief.

Rendering unto Caesar that which is Caesar's and unto God what is God's was mostly what each member of the CIM described this time in Belgium to be. In fact, the leaders of CIM/AIMM decided that all of the funds being channeled to the ministry from Belgium would in fact be placed into a fund for capital expenditures. What that meant is that the funding would help to build more schools, more hospitals and clinics, and yes, even some churches in areas where there was a need. That is the financial discipline that the country of Congo has rarely seen. Just think about this example of financial responsibility that has paid dividends for the people of Congo for more than fifty years in the mission stations that have long been turned over to the Congolese.

Back to Lodema in the classroom

We mentioned Lodema's love for art and painting earlier. Although this was something that was included in the normal curriculum for the students at Nyanga's Miodi School it was not sufficient to meet the needs of all the kids. There were three students she discovered who had almost as great an interest in art and painting. This meant

Three such students who excelled and worked on their own time painting are: Mutombo M'Panya, Leonard Kakesa, and Andre Mwina

that she would purchase art supplies from her own funds to see them enjoy painting and succeed. Archie Graber would find time on his journeys to the city and around the country to also buy art supplies for Lodema's students, knowing how important this was to each of them.

All three of these young men became significant contributors to society as adults, and yet their memories of Lodema taking special time to order art supplies to teach them the importance of using their talents and creativity was never forgotten. In fact, Mutombo was part of the group who revisited Congo in 2012 for the Centennial Celebration of one hundred years of ministry there that began with Mennonite

Missionaries in 1912. In reflecting on what he learned about art and its impact on his life, here are his own words: *She gave me some confidence in artistic things so that I could read art, much the same as reading music. This helped me develop perspectives that carried over into other areas.* (Mutombo later studied in the USA and became a professor of Mathematics at Sonoma State University in California.)

There are countless stories about some other aspects of Lodema's reputation in the classroom. Almost every interview would include

Photo of school buildings in Nyanga by author, July, 2012

some or all of the descriptions like, strongly disciplined; punctual to a fault; holding high expectations; caring about the success of all the students; and of course going the extra mile. The reason that punctuality is an unusual trait to be praised by the Congolese students of Lodema is to understand a term we call *African time.*

African time

On my first trip to Africa in 2001, we took a basketball team to Kenya to play against high school and local teams in the Greater Mombasa area. I had been warned that there was such a thing as *African Time* and I should not let it bother me.

"No problem, nothing will bother me," I insisted!

The test came when our team got to the very first official game that was to start at 1:00 PM. Our team arrived at 12:15, and when unloading the bus, we found no one. The court was covered with debris, and I didn't even recognize it as a court at all. The local missionary didn't say a word but went and found eight or nine branches which he formed into a broom, and handed it to our players to start sweeping off the court. Yes, there was some concrete underneath all the dirt and cow dung, but the metal rims had no nets and were hanging crooked on the poles. We decided to try to repair them, and since we brought some extra nets, we hung those too.

It got to be 1:30 and still no school kids or players from the school had arrived. We were all trying to be less bothered by the idea of punctuality. It was even harder to dismiss the thought of stealing time from others when you do not respect being on time. I was to the point of formulating how I might add time theft into my sermon if I would have a chance to preach. "Thou Shalt NOT Steal my TIME!" How about that for a sermon title? We flew 7,000 miles to play a game of basketball and these students can't walk from their school or homes to get here on time?

Slowly a few kids started to trickle in here and there, and soon there were six of them and then seven but still no coach. How can you be a coach and set this example? It is now 2:30 and our players are tired of warming up, and also wondering why they are here as well. Eventually, the coaches and players all arrived and they apologized for all the things they had to do before coming to the game. The fact that they did show up, played a competitive game, and represented themselves and their school was more than enough. All of this took place without this ugly American's moralizing sermon on punctuality.

This attitude about time being a movable target was never part of Lodema's classroom. She and the other teachers at Miodi became known for their demanding expectations for both punctuality and for overcoming the mindset sometimes referred to as *Africa Time*.

When individual school days were over, Lodema routinely opened her front yard to the kids to come by and study or be part of Bible Studies that she would host. One of the reasons that Momma Kanemu was so well respected is because she, along with the rest of the CIM staff, consistently viewed and genuinely treated the students with sincere respect. How beautiful if the world could adopt the same respect for the people of Congo even today.

In interview after interview, Lodema's students would recall with a smile on their face that you just never wanted to be late to class. She was not a large or imposing woman who would frighten the kids with physical punishment, but she was unyielding when it came to setting standards and expecting people to live up to them. One of the pastors indicated that when Lodema asked him a question, it was always built with an expected answer but also with the challenge to think beyond the obvious. The future teachers that graduated from the schools in Nyanga became equipped with both knowledge and ideals that exceeded the normal standards. Yes, Lodema would be proud to see her students today!

The school at Nyanga serves over two hundred students each year to help place more professionals into Congolese society. Lodema would be even more pleased to see how many of her students are preparing the youth of Nyanga and Kasai Province for productive lives and have influence in all parts of Congo.

Freedom Generation Finds Their Way

"I am sure that he is able to guard until that Day what has been entrusted to me."
II Timothy 1:12b (RSV)

Gauging the successes of those who grew up in Congo after the country became independent can best be seen through three examples. The Congolese suffered from poor schools, decayed roads, poor access to medical facilities, and inefficient markets for their goods. There are many men and women from the southern parts of Congo that were students and beneficiaries of the missionary outreach of AIMM/CIM who were able to rise above such problems.

Most of the world never gets past Kinshasa as their focal point of what Congo is all about. Consequently, most people do not even know about places like Tshikapa, Mbuji Mayi, and villages like Nyanga in the Southern Kasai Province of the Democratic Republic of Congo. The visibility of these places and the people who studied at the Mennonite Mission stations is also very low. We will not make that mistake.

Some of the greatest success stories have their roots in the schools and churches of these people of Congo. The students from those years are the forbearers of the parents, church leaders, and community leaders of today.

During the Centennial Celebration in 2012, one person after another came to be interviewed to talk about their schooling and training they received from Lodema and the other missionaries. Many of them are pastors, business leaders, and homemakers, but they all agreed their education had changed their lives. It is not difficult to connect the dots on why such changes were possible. Educational advancements created these legacies and the men and women who administered and taught in these schools have left legacies that will never be fully measured except by God. Three legacies became apparent:

- Three students attend college in the United States (1960's)
- Girls are included in the formal education process (1970's)
- Women become ordained as ministers in the Mennonite denominations of Congo (2012)

Three young men leave the Congo to go to the USA for college

Freeman, South Dakota, gets pretty cold in the winter. Convincing Robert Ilunga and Maurice Ilunga, along with Theodore Mbualungu to attend Freeman Junior College to begin their collegiate studies in North America was an even bigger challenge than convincing the *Happy Singers* to go to Belgium. This small Jr. College in the southernmost part of the Dakotas was a Mennonite School dedicated to helping students transition from high school to college. The educators and sponsors for these young men thought this to be a perfect place for them to learn English and the American lifestyle.

Lodema was an eye witness to many of her own students moving into responsible adulthood as they survived Independence, the Kwilu Rebellion, and a selfish dictator. How appropriate for the young Congolese students to attend their first school outside of Africa at an institution by the name of *Freeman*! Many received scholarships to study outside of Africa, while others were able to attend the University of Congo during the 1970's. The most powerful contribution of the schools in Nyanga and the other mission stations are the pastors, doctors, and teachers who now have become the leaders in Congo.

Many of these professionals who have attended the various mission schools over the years end up choosing to live in the larger cities. Others choose to live in a foreign country where jobs and working conditions are more lucrative. Even today, living in Congo is not easy. Raising your children to attend schools that sometimes are barely functional requires patience and a strong will. Congolese who have spent time in the USA and Canada often end up staying there as do their children. This is both understandable and unfortunate as these people who are so needed in the Congo choose to stay in their new environment.

When Robert, Maurice, and Theodore took on this challenge to study abroad, there was more than a little speculation on just how they would handle the academic and social challenges. The USA was still in the very early stages of the Civil Rights Movement, and Dr. Martin Luther King's March on Washington took place about the same time as these young men were learning English. They could speak conversationally as they had done when the singers were in Brussels, but to handle normal classroom work in an American university required a leap of faith and a lot of hard work. Lodema had no doubts that if the young men were able to develop their language skills, the rest of their educational experiences would fall into place.

Fall into place it did! All three of these new students achieved at the top of the class in English at Freeman and then matriculated to different schools to finish their college degrees. The societal pressures that surrounded not only black students from Congo, but also African Americans were that they were unable to perform at very high levels intellectually and academically. This was a stereotype that Lodema encountered so often when she would talk about her work in Congo. The sense that she was doing something dramatic by pulling the kids up to higher standards would set her off. She knew that given any normal classroom structure and quality teaching, the kids she was working with from the Congo had every bit as much academic potential as any she had seen in America.

The generosity and vision that coupled together to help jump start these students and many others to keep going with their education began to have an impact. Theodore graduated from Taylor University in Upland, Indiana, and returned to Congo in the mid-sixties to take a position within the church conference at Stanleyville. Maurice earned a degree from Freeman, and then finished his Bachelor of Science degree at Eastern Mennonite, in Harrisonburg, Virginia, (near Washington D.C.), and also returned to help in the schools and churches of Congo. Robert finished his work at Bluffton College in Bluffton, Ohio, and eventually returned to also be a source of strength and leadership in his home country. Robert was instrumental in being one of the Congolese church leaders who took over from the missionaries in 1971.

These were watershed events almost as significant as the Independence movement and the World's Fair. In many ways they were more significant because they paved the way, setting an example that young African men could study and achieve academic success in a modern setting. The stereotyping that prevailed from Europe to North America about the potential for black people was slowly melting away every time a Robert, Maurice, and Theodore stepped through the door and excelled in the classroom. This has not stopped all of the struggles that people of color still experience around the world. What these missionaries to Congo did and proved to the world was truly remarkable. What the students did in turn was even more remarkable!

Perhaps girls could benefit from attending school

Another significant event happened in Congo when the mission teachers and administrators decided to start a girl's school in Nyanga.

Lodema was both excited and yet apprehensive about the prospect of teaching these young women. She was used to working with the boys and seeing them turn into young men, but the African traditions for women were deeply ingrained. Congo, as with most of Africa, is a pater-

Leonie Khelendende, the only girl in Nyanga to be allowed in the classroom to help her three brothers. Picture provided by Wanda Short from Lodema's archives

92

nalistic society, and the importance and potential for girls and women was very limited. How could she deal with the ideals of the excitement and limitless creativity of the human minds of these girls when that might be in conflict with their culture?

In the very first year of the Lycee Miodi School for girls, these fears proved to be un- founded and quickly dismissed. Lodema and the entire mission staff found these young women who started to go on to advanced studies to be every bit as serious as the young men. There had been a young woman who paved the way for the idea of a school for  girls. The first female graduate of the Nyanga Schools was a young woman named Leonie Khelendende. As you can see in the picture on the previous page, she is the only girl in the class. She was unaware of her role as a path finder and merely worked at her studies oblivious that all of her classmates were boys.

Because she had so many brothers that she cared for and had worked with in her family surroundings, she was not aware of any of the world's gender issues. No one knew for sure how she got into school, but the best guess was that she was there to help her brothers. She had no idea that it would take another fifty or so years from her time at the Nyanga Schools before a woman would become a pastor in the Mennonite Church of Congo. Yes, many people remember her as a helpful supportive young woman. Little did she know at the time she was also a pioneer.

The students were challenged to see their upside and their potential while those who would dismiss this country and its people would have to admit that given opportunity, they could succeed. It is still going on today. If you walk the cities and countryside of the southern provinces in the DRC, you will find students of Momma Kanemu and her colleagues. The work of the church has multiplied by a factor of ten or more as the Congolese are totally in control. In 2012, the Mennonites of Congo even started to ordain women to the ministry.

Martini Janz (also known as Mama Kin'a Kivule) was another missionary who took a special interest in the girls of the village. She would often listen to their joys and concerns and offer quiet insight and advice when given the chance. One of the young girls who sought her advice on many issues was Marie Bongesa who later married Louis Mukanzu who was one of the Brussels *Happy Singers*. Their fifty year old daughter, Odette Mukole found Martini in Canada during the Centennial observance at their EMC church. Odette was studying at the Mennonite University in Winnipeg and was told by her mother to find Mama Kin'a Kivule.

Madam Bercy with Dwight Short at the Kalonda Bible Institute, July 2012 (picture provided by author)

Martini had a flashback to 1956, when Bongesa came to her veranda to ask Martini if she would help her to be baptized. She asked her if she had made a decision to follow Christ in her life and Bongesa said "YES!" The memories started rolling in for Martini as she could see Louis, Odette's handsome father, in his powder blue suit preparing with the others to go to Belgium to sing. She also saw in this one young descendant of Louis and Marie, the embodiment of what it meant for women of the Congo to seek higher education. Even at fifty years of age, Odette wanted to finish her college degree and find more positive ways to serve the Lord. That is a legacy not to be forgotten or ignored!

Girls become Women; Women become Pastors

Women in positions of control and power in the entire continent of Africa is unusual. Add the traditions of the evangelical church to that equation, and the likelihood of women leading the churches in Africa has taken some time. But once again, the power of God and the strength of academic training have seen women who could teach future pastors in the Bible Training Institute, but not be empowered to be a pastor. That too is changing as several very competent women are being ordained including the very first one, Madame Mimi Kanku. Seen in the picture below with her husband being honored at a service in Mbuji Mayi, she represents the culmination of the work of so many people who have laid a foundation in the schools of the Congo.

Originally, this foundation was due to the missionaries, but today the students of those missionaries are taking the leadership roles and running forward with great passion and vision for the future. In a

Madam Bercy with other pastors and leaders at Kalonda, July 2012

country that often breaks down and does not work, the work God has ordained in this part of Congo flourishes. Credit also goes to Benjamin Mubenga, President of the Evangelical Mennonite Church of Congo (CEM) and Adolphe Komuesa Kalunga, President of the Mennonite Community of Congo (CMCO) as they have seen the importance of breaking with gender traditions. Their vision and hope for the future includes women in the ministry because they believe more will come to know Christ as a result of this calling for people of both genders.

During Mimi Kanku Mayi's seven hour ordination service, there was an anointing time and a sprinkling of powder that symbolized entry to the ministry. There was also a calling to show that she was now a servant to the entire body of believers, and not just married to her family. Surrounded by nineteen other candidates for ordination, they joined in prayer to ask the Holy Spirit to use them for God's glory.

In September 2013, just a little more than a year later, another woman, Madame Bercy Mundedi, was ordained to the ministry after answering a calling that started at her birth in Nyanga. Her father was a student of Lodema's and had excelled in her classes. When her father was preparing to start his advanced studies, he was able to earn extra money working at the missionary home for the single women of the Nyanga Mission Station. Lodema happily baby sat the young infant now known as the Sister Bercy Mundedi, a pastor in the Mennonite Church of Congo.

Not being totally aware of all this history, this author approached Madam Bercy during the Centennial Celebration in 2012 to share some thoughts. It was important to tell her that Lodema would be very happy to see such a competent and effective woman in a position of leadership. She had already taught for many years at the Kalonda Bible Institute and indeed had trained many of the pastors already in the field. That is when she shared the story of how she not only knew of Lodema through her father's stories, but also had been inspired by so many of the women who had worked alongside Lodema and set such a wonderful example for her to emulate.

When Lodema, and the other missionaries from the AIMM/CIM, left the church to the Congolese in the mid-1980's, there were about 400 churches and 25,000 believers. In 2012, there were over 30,000 churches and 250,000 believers. Countless numbers of the pastors of those churches were students of Lodema and the other missionary workers from those original mission stations of the Congo Inland Mission. Even more of their students are acting as leaders in the same churches and communities where they live as Christians attempting just like Christians all over the world to serve the Lord.

One unintended consequence of the Independence of Congo was the earlier than expected transfer of power from the missionaries to the Congolese. God has blessed that transfer and fusion in ways no one could have imagined. Thank God for those with vision and courage to trust that it would work this well!

God's Calling Today (Are you an Isaac?)

"Therefore go and make disciples of all nations..." Matthew 28:19 (NIV)

Congo is a different place today from the world of the mission societies of the twentieth century. The need for mission workers has never been greater, but the openness and the needs of the society are quite different. People are still hungry to hear the Gospel Message of Jesus's Saving Grace, but the messengers must deliver the Good News in a different way. Many churches would prefer the message be delivered by a Congolese pastor or leader. The schools are still in even greater need of teachers, but the society is calling for those teachers to be Congolese as well.

In the Mennonite denominations of Congo, there is a unique openness to influence and guidance from traditional missionary societies. The Africa Inter-Mennonite Mission (AIMM) has succeeded in combining the best of the foundational leaders and the enthusiasm of the current Congolese leaders. The memories of Lodema Short, Archie Graber, Jim Bertsche and MANY MANY others are still honored and revered alongside the early Congolese patriarchs such as Pastor Matthew Kazadi.

Testing whether we are open to God's calling is like placing ourselves on the altar periodically to seek the Lord as to whether we are being used in the place of HIS choice. Just as Abraham was willing to sacrifice his only son Isaac, based on the Lord's calling, we too must be open to hear God's voice through our total being. In fact, real obedience is to be an Isaac and crawl up on the altar ourselves to say to God, "Here I am, take me!"

The missionaries we have seen from Lodema's time were often challenged by other missionaries or perhaps responded during a church altar call to become a servant of God. That *calling* was extended beyond one's vocation to include geography, family ties, and any other aspect of one's life that would hold you back from being all you could be as a servant of God.

One of the most famous choruses that was used during the altar calls at the Billy Graham Evangelistic Crusades is *Just As I Am*. The call to missions is the same. Just as you are, God can use you! But how? Isn't it true that many countries don't want foreign missionaries anymore? Even in the African countries that are in need of teachers, doctors, and nurses, there is an outcry that these tasks should be done by people of their own country. That is true, but it does not preclude opportunities for specialized short and intermediate term projects that can make a difference. Think about the following areas of need:

- Church building and repair of existing churches. Many need to be built but even more of them are in disrepair and in need

of refurbishing. The church in Nyanga is in need of repair; no services can be held there now.

- Specialized teachers and teacher training including teaching English as a second language. This may be done during summers or vacations.
- Advancing entrepreneurship and teaching greater economic independence as in the photo below of a farming operation in Ukraine by Aslan Management Group. Hundreds of small farms were joined together to make a twenty-five thousand acre farming operation to obtain both critical mass and economy of scale. Many of the same farmers who leased their land (usually less than twenty acres per farmer) to Aslan came to work for them and would be responsible for a tractor, combine, or building.

Ukraine farms in Kherson Province of Ukraine, 2007 (photo by author)

- Fostering ecumenical unity with other denominations that allows a school or hospital to survive and grow in strategic areas of need. A great example of this is the Albert Schweitzer Hospital in Lambarene, Gabon. The Albert Schweitzer Society today has built an endowment to send doctors and nurses to maintain the facility with ecumenical support. There are more worthy projects waiting for people who will answer the calling of God.

- Developing a network for Micro Loans; planning for small businesses and providing capital for those willing to work to provide for their families but in need of capital to start or further their business.

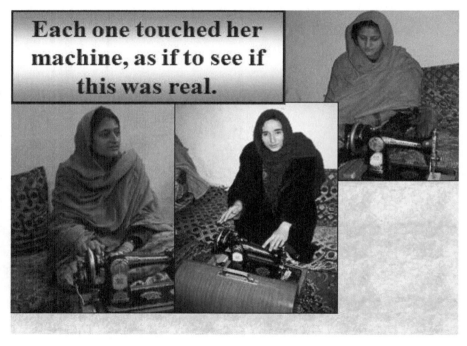

Afghan widows receive a loan to produce sewn goods with their sewing machines to avoid being an outcast from their families and society.

- Youth programs that may include presenting a Vacation Bible School or doing a drama presentation with young people. Music programs for youth could include both instrumental and choral events.

- Scholarship programs that would help people in need study in an institution that you might have some influence in arranging. If you have financial resources and want to remain anonymous, you can work through Christian Community Foundations like *In His Steps Foundation* or the *National Christian Foundation.*
- Building and repairing homes, schools, orphanages, libraries, any structure this is considered vital in a community that needs outside help
- Sports Evangelism for both athletes and coaches. Take extra equipment and supplies with you as the schools and kids you serve have never seen a basketball net or even a real soccer ball.

Hanging new nets in Kenya before a basketball clinic 2001 (photo by author)

- Let me take your place ministries…offer to give two weeks of your time to give someone in a similar service as you a vacation. Check with your denominational missions groups to see if your skills would fit with some of their full time staff that are serving in difficult and demanding parts of the world with no time off.

- Laundry projects where teams go into neighborhoods and clean people's dirty clothes and offer dignity to them. These projects are usually available in your own community or very close to home in local laundromats.

- Clinics for teaching all kinds of skills such as soccer, basketball, football, baseball, etc. The impromptu soccer clinic that you see below attracted over four hundred kids from around the city of Tshikapa during the 2012 Centennial celebration. Many of the kids who attended this event touched and kicked a real soccer ball for the first time in their life. You can give of yourself and teach many more lessons and experiences while sharing the Good News of Christ when doing such clinics.

Soccer Clinic in Tshikapa, Congo, July 2012. The man with the soccer ball is Robert Irundu, Youth Pastor for Mennonite Church of Congo, members of Derksen Family who wowed the 400 youth who were part of the clinic to learn team work on the soccer field. (photo by author)

- Medical Missions both in general and specific in nature. The health needs of people around the world continue to increase as diseases and sanitary conditions require attention. Serving in areas where the churches and mission organizations can provide the structure to meet as many people and patients in a short time period can maximize the value of doctors and nurses who are willing to help on short term projects.
- Flying airplanes, driving vehicles, bringing expertise to work sites and mission stations around the corner or around the world. Mission networks and denominational mission leaders can help find these areas of service.
- Water projects; finding ways to drill wells & bring new water sources to villages and communities. Drilling wells and giving training in water usage along with pumping systems can make a big difference in a short time.

Several men carry water more than two miles to fill a cistern. (photo by author)

Your turn: **what is God calling you to do**? Our list has barely scratched the surface of ways you can serve the Lord by offering yourself as a servant. Working in nursing homes, food banks, hunger centers, blood banks, and just offering to visit people in their homes is a great way to be an Isaac.

God has not stopped calling people to do His work. Just like Lodema responded in 1945 to the idea that her training as a teacher could be used in a place like the Belgian Congo, God can use you today in the same way. Your training and experience is not an accident. You do not have to become someone that you are not to go somewhere unusual to serve God as a missionary. But just like Isaac crawling back up on the altar, we must be willing to go where God calls us. Part of our faith journey is to trust God that when we do follow such a path that is different from the world's idea, then we will receive confirmation and encouragement for having done so.

The Power of Short-Term Missions

One of the first short term sports missions that we were able to be part of was a trip to Mombasa, Kenya, with a high school basketball team. The team was just starting to get some unity when we were confronted with some minor dissention about playing time among our players. After our first two games, we had very cordial exchanges between our players and the players from the other team. But none of our opponents or any of the people watching us seemed to respond to our Christian testimonies. At our evening devotions that night, one of the coaches, Frank Stretar, could sense that there was a division between us and the Lord in our manner and demeanor.

He had tears in his eyes as he started to pray for our team that night. Each word came out with more emotion and passion as he prayed. We could sense that what he was praying for was our humility. We had not intended to be superior or arrogant, but that must have been what we conveyed to those we intended to help. As Frank slowly got to his knees, one by one we all got to our knees and humbled ourselves before God to seek his will in both our jump shots and our persona. Every day from that night through the rest of the trip we saw almost one hundred people come to know Christ.

As our trip in Kenya came to a close, the missionary families in the Mombasa area started to come to our games. The local newspaper heard about our team and they came to our games and wrote stories about us totally unsolicited. The top basketball program in the city invited us to play them on the only indoor basketball court in the city of Mombasa. We accepted their invitation and were able to play before a thousand people who came to the game. After the game we left our basketball shoes and all our remaining equipment for the schools and teams to use along with our witness for Christ.

Yes, we did win most of our games for those of you who are reading this and want to know about wins and losses. But the face of Oliver and our two Muslim bus drivers will be forever etched in my mind. They came to love what we were doing and saw these kids coming to know Christ, and they too were coming close to making a decision for Christ but could not quite do it right then and there. Like King Agrippa in the Bible, they were almost persuaded but not quite. Maybe next year, we thought…

In our minds, we had already decided that we had been so successful and so well received that we would come back to Mombasa every year. This was in June of 2001. When 9/11 happened we found this door to team sports ministry in the predominantly Muslim city of Mombasa to be closed. The very first rule of ministry and missions is that **God opens and closes doors and hearts.** Don't think that you can be anything but faithful. If you are being called to a place or a task, it will not always be there nor will it always be the same as you think it will be.

The second rule of missions is **never underestimate what God can do with committed and sincere servants.** When we gathered in Mombasa that last night to talk about the things that happened, Stan, the local missionary who was also the local basketball coach at Mombasa Baptist HS, was all choked up about the previous ten days.

We thought he probably got this way whenever he was saying goodbye to his guests. We had taken an offering among the team and given him an extra gift to say thanks for all they had done for us when he started with these crocodile tears. The offering wasn't that much, but we didn't think he ought to cry over it.

"We haven't seen anyone come to know Christ here in over two years!" he sobbed.

It is easy to assume that every day people are becoming Christians and dedicating their lives to the Lord in every place where missionaries are working.

The third rule of missions is **if God is calling, just go!** We had no idea that God could use a basketball team as a catalyst for renewal and encouragement for the missionaries themselves. Just the living of everyday lives and raising families can tire the most dedicated missionary.

There will always be detractors, or those who will ask you why would you go to a faraway place when there are hungry and unsaved people right at home? My answer to them is that I am happy if they see an opportunity to serve near home and maybe that should be *their* calling. When I return home from the place God is asking me to serve now, I will offer, God willing, to go with them in ministry to that place as well. It is not that God has stopped calling, it appears that we as believers have stopped listening. As Lodema once painted her picture and entitled it, *Will he Hear?* God must be asking the same question about His Church worldwide. Will they hear Me? If they do, Will they follow?

How will I know where to go? God will provide both the indication of need and the places where the people are open and ready to receive you and your gifts. You may be called to plant seeds of the Kingdom while others will water them. You will not always be at the harvest but God knows what is needed more than any of us. Just being faithful to the call is all we can do!

Being in Kenya to see kids ready to receive Christ in their life was great preparation for going to Morocco when all we could do is be Christ's witness by being there. God calls people to go to faraway places and also to serve in our homes and neighborhoods.

Many churches today would rather build huge sanctuaries and physical plants that look more like an ivory palace than to spend the same proportional amount on the Great Commission. Supporting missions can be something to clear one's conscience by observing it once a year then budgeting nominal funds to outreach. Mission budgets have been the victim of major cuts when times are bad because the physical buildings take so much cost and priority to maintain. It does appear that we often break rule #2 by trying to see what God can do about stopping the roof from leaking in our gigantic churches compared to the same money being spent to bring people to eternal knowledge of our Savior. Just think of all of that untapped potential!

If God is calling, just go!

Congo's Future & the Hope of the People

"To the question whether I am a pessimist or an optimist, I answer that my knowledge is pessimistic, but my willing and hoping are optimistic…But however much concerned I was at the problem of the misery in the world, I never let myself get lost in broodings over it. I always held firmly to the thought that each one of us can do a little to bring some portion of it to an end." (Albert Schweitzer from his essay entitled, "Out of My Life and Thought")

Two of the World's Fair *Happy Singers* sat together talking about the current state of affairs in the Congo during their interview in July, 2012. Military intervention was being attempted against the rebel forces, *The M23*, by Congolese Government troops in the Northeastern Congo area often referred to as the conflict minerals region. Theodore Mbualungu and Maurice Ilunga talked about the possibility of the Government troops actually getting control of the region. Maurice was not very optimistic that they would be successful, but Theodore believed that this time would be different, and he believed they would gain enough leverage to restore order. I sat in total silence wanting to hear how this discussion would work out and who would be most convincing.

Theodore was quite passionate as he cited the recent elections and the changes he was seeing just living in Kinshasa as a sign that the country and its government were changing for the better. Maurice asked how Theodore saw any positive changes, to which Theodore replied, "I just believe the time has come for better things to happen to our country!"

There is a new wave of people who believe this is the time for positive change. Many economists agree with Theodore, and they believe the resource rich Congo could be compared to Brazil as one of the countries that could turn into a dynamic growth area in the 21st Century. This will require more than just extracting and refining the minerals and substances from the rich deposits that lie inside the Congo's natural resource treasures. This will not only require intentional policies and planning arrangements that utilize the country's wealth of resources, but also training its wealth of willing workers and people. Many people believe this process has already begun even though progress looks slow to the outside world.

Advancing the cause of Congo will require help from within the country and from outside forces. Attempts by the United Nations have yielded mixed results. Super powers such as the USA, China, and Russia could have some impact if it can be channeled and controlled by a stronger Congolese government that also includes tighter controls on bribes and graft. There will also have to be parallel efforts on the part of global businesses and private industry who wish to do business in Congo. Their activities and the revenue created by their involvement must include a portion that goes to the infrastructure of the Congo.

Most of the roads in Congo are in need of repair. The trains, buses, and transportation systems are out of date and in need of capital investment. Most of the schools, hospitals, and government facilities are much worse across the nation than they were when funded and operated by the colonial authorities and missionaries from the 1960's and 1970's. Health standards and disease control is a major problem in almost every city and village in the Democratic Republic of Congo.

The most modern building in Kinshasa is the National government office building, which was built as a gift by China. This exemplifies the policy of China to help, but also maintain strict controls on funding to make sure the projects are completed as planned. Western foreign aid programs have a history of lining a local politician's pocket instead of building the roads or buildings they were intended to fund.

The pessimists would have an easy time recording the events of the post-colonial period of Congo while the optimists would have to work harder to find their examples for why the glass is half full. A recent book, Congo Masquerade by Theodore Trefon offers detailed examples of how efforts to help Congo have been met with mixed results. In addition to the conditions described in the lead paragraph, it would be wrong to not include the role of *conflict minerals* in the pessimistic side of the ledger. Tantalum (also known as coltan), tin, tungsten, and now gold, have been the source of great wealth and are found in the mines of Congo. There are other minerals that are significantly important to the world that are also mined in Congo, but the conflict minerals have led to many deaths, forced labor, and refugee elements when the tribal militias force their way into areas and force the residents out. The US passed a law under the *Dodd Frank Amendment* that required verification of the sources for such minerals to try to eliminate the unscrupulous forces from this equation.

The technological revolution that has swept the world since 1990 has brought computers, tablets, and of course cell phones into the hands of millions of people and has created an insatiable demand for the substance coltan. Every device being produced requires a small amount of this substance, and the tribal militias figured out this demand fast enough to take over mining operations to a large extent in northeastern Congo. Often referred to as the Kivu region, this area has been a war zone between the government forces of Congo and the tribal militias made up of former government soldiers, soldiers of fortune from Ruanda and Uganda, and many young recruits from conquered villages and jungle warriors.

Not only has this torn at the very soul of the people of Congo, it is an economic disaster for them as well. The mineral profits end up in the pockets of a few people who buy more guns and weapons to keep their dynasty in place so the world can buy cheaper cell phones and computers while they get rich. Here is a summary of how The *Enough Project Congo* describes this issue:

> *The war in eastern Congo began in the early 1990s and continues to this day. It has encompassed two international wars—from 1996 to 1997 and 1998 to 2003—and multiple invasions from neighboring countries, with combatants from many armed groups, both foreign and domestic. While Congo has abundant natural*

resources, it is also the world's poorest country per capita, according to the United Nations. Congo is also home to the largest and most expensive U.N. peacekeeping mission in the world, MONUSCO, which has more than 20,000 personnel and an annual budget of $1.4 billion. The eastern part of the country is plagued by instability, as militias continue to wreak havoc on the population. Meanwhile, the conflict gets very little coverage by the international media.

The conflict in Congo is notorious for serious violations of human rights, including violence against women and the use of child soldiers. Since 1996 the International Rescue Committee has calculated that approximately 5.4 million people have died from war-related causes. In 2012 Congo ranked lowest on the United Nations Human Development Index.

For many years, people from the western countries have been dismissive about the existence and the cause of these problems of Congo as something that takes place in a distant country. Why be concerned about something that we are not responsible for and did not cause? This has become a hollow argument when we realize that the technology we enjoy is a byproduct of this very problem. How many times have we seen a better cell phone or computer come onto the market that caused us to throw away our old device and buy the new one? The fact that new devices could continue to be sold at such low prices is a combination of both technological advances and also the cheap purchase of substances like coltan. People will stand in long lines to purchase new cell phones and devices, but very few are standing in lines to defend those who are enslaved in the coltan mines.

There are companies like the financial services firm, *Everence*, who have staged public campaigns to ask their followers to ask their cell phone providers to only sell products from conflict free zones. It has not made a major difference in the market place but the presence of *Dodd Frank* and mostly the efforts of many corporations in the technology industry to verify their sources, will make a difference. None of this will have the desired impact on the country itself if the Congolese leadership cannot change the culture of bribes and dishonesty that has been planted and festered for more than a hundred years.

The sources of pessimism

The modern source of inhumanity in Congo is traceable to King Leopold II when in the late 1800's he convinced world leaders that he would help civilize and modernize the Free State of Congo. Leopold was allowed to proceed with this process under agreements that the US and European powers approved. The civilizing and humanitarian ideals did not last long. Rather than peaceful ideals, he quickly taught his soldiers how to brutalize another human being by chopping off hands to save bullets.

He profited personally with the sale of latex for rubber tires at the start of the automotive revolution. Profits from the sale of elephant tusks for ivory piano keys and jewelry were almost as significant.

The same tradition goes on in the conflict mineral mining operations of Congo one hundred and thirty years later. If you need workers in the mines, recruit with force and fear, and use the same tactics toward labor relations to keep output at needed levels.

Leopold also laid the groundwork for what the Belgians took to an even greater art form. This was the inferiority complex that race played in determining status both by translating Europeans and Westerners as superior, and then the most disgusting of all ideas, that the shade of pigmentation also could be used as a factor for status. This was played out in the country of Ruanda to an even greater extent than Congo, but because of the eruption that took place in Ruanda between the Hutu's (darker skinned) and Tutsi (lighter skinned), it impacted Congo as well. These are complex issues that we are not going to treat adequately in this text other than to point out the origins of these conflicts must be recognized if progress is to come in the future.

You may recall our discussion of Mobutu in earlier chapters, who arrived in power thanks to the US and other western powers, who thought him more controllable than his previous boss, Patrice Lumumba. For over thirty years, Mobutu lined his pockets with incredible wealth, but he also added a curse to the country as his personal legacy often referred to as *Article 15*. This segment from *In the Footsteps of Mr. Kurtz* tells us how this system was supposed to work for everyone:

...when Mobutu, addressing a ruling party conference, acknowledged that it was acceptable to "teal a little," as long as the theft remained within limits. By the 1990's, Article 15 *was the sardonic thread running through the fabric of Zairian society, the raison d'etre of a leader, a government an entire regime. Prime ministers came and went, each of them doling out civil service jobs for the boys. There were official drivers for ministries without cars, switchboard operators for departments without phones, secretaries without typewriters. They were paid an average of $6 a month but hung on nonetheless in the hope that one day the economy would revive and they would get what they were owed in back wages.*

For teachers it was pass marks they could dole out to ambitious pupils in exchange for groceries. For soldiers who rented themselves out to private businessmen or restaurants as bodyguards, it was the promise of security.

So *Article 15* was a reference to an ambiguous place in the Constitution of Zaire that never existed but allowed for people to *legally* steal from others. Mobutu thought that if he allowed others to do what he was doing with the corporate and government interests who were extracting natural resources from the country and the country's coffers, then he thought that would allow him to stay in power. For that part, he was right. But most of his ability to stay in power revolved around his close ties to the military leaders and his ability to make sure the skids were greased sufficiently to keep his enemies at bay.

In this society with such deep roots in violence and bribery, why would anyone want to take on the optimistic point of view? That is the western dilemma that we must all lay aside. If you could meet the people of Congo, you would know why it easy to have reasons for optimism. The world is stuck on these pessimistic ideas because that is usually what they see, read, and hear from the traditional sources of information. Other than this book, when have you last read about or heard accounts of happenings in Tshikapa, Mbuji Mayi, or Nyanga?

God's people will make a difference

When you meet the people on the street and those who are part of the leadership of Congo, there is a new generation on the move. They come from many backgrounds and religious traditions, but the vast majority names the name of Christ as their Savior. That alone should make us optimistic, but we know that money, greed, and temptation are also hard to overcome when even believers are placed in a position of power. What are some of the things that would make a difference in Congo? Our list would have to include the following:

Women of Congo

As we saw in the ordination of women among the Mennonite denominations of Congo, the education and upward mobility of women will have a huge impact on the future of the country. Being able to place more women in the schools and places of need within the infrastructure of Congo will raise productivity and compliance for their children. They are ready, and the support given by United Nations relief agencies will lead to more positive roles. There are disgustingly high estimates of the number of women in Congo who have suffered sexual attacks and rapes during the wars and violence of the recent decades. Having survived this and still moving forward is a testament to the spirit of these women of Congo. Do NOT underestimate what they can do with God's help. Many cries for help have seemed to go unanswered in this hellish atmosphere that has existed in parts of Congo, but there are so many examples of those who have come to the aid and support of those in need, that the end of the story has not been written.

There is also a universal understanding and support network that is building: "Women all laugh the same, cry the same, talk about many of the same things that we want to do with our lives," says Aisha Bain, advocacy adviser for the Democratic Republic of the Congo at *International Rescue Committee*. Despite vastly different circumstances between Western women and those in Goma, eastern DRC – many of whom

Open air church in Kinshasa, mother and daughters worshipping (photo by the author)

have been displaced by fighting – Bain says there is also much that they share.

Military congruence with societal needs

The military has played a pivotal role in the Congo dating all the way back to when King Leopold II formed his local law enforcement group. Subsequently, militia groups have been formed from tribal groups to build and protect property and borders within the country from the time of Independence in 1960 to the present. The intent and purpose of these groups has rarely been to protect the public at large, but to protect the ability of the top ranking officials of each group to enforce a state of fear and compliance in order for them to profit from either slave labor or illegal seizure and sale of precious minerals. When a police or military force can be trusted with the common good of the people, there will be significant progress on all fronts.

Men of Congo

The men have been the dominant force in a patriarchal society such as Congo. This is still going to be true going forward, but there are reasons to think there could be serious changes coming. The forces for change will actually be the education and training of their wives and sisters. Men will see the need for sharing power as a sign of strength.

Vice Governor, Bruno Kazadi Bukasa, (with the microphone) of Kasai Province Congo, also a Pastor, shares his dream for all his fellow citizens to know Jesus Christ; Rod Hollinger Janzen, Executive Dir. AIMM; Pastor Joseph Mubenga, President, EMC Congo (Photo by the author taken in Mbuji Mayi, July 2012)

As Christians are able to gain greater leadership opportunities, it is possible to see a change in the perception of both men and women and the importance of children in the Congolese society. Men will want to stand for the right things!

Government stability and integrity that would include peaceful resolution of border disputes

The biggest obstacle currently being contested is the northeastern area of Congo that borders Ruanda and Uganda. Military units with government backing from these bordering countries are still exacting revenge from conflicts that are smoldering from many years ago, and the people of these areas are caught in the middle. That prevents many kids from getting to school, and most people are unable to access even the most basic medical care.

Refugee Resolution

The same violent and war torn events have caused great misplacement of people from their homes and villages. Some method of helping those in the refugee areas to start anew while others may find it possible to return to their homes is necessary to the dissolution of the refugee camps.

Proper training and recruitment of teachers, doctors, and professional services for both the cities and the country's outlying villages

Restoration of schools, hospitals, and medical services

Partnership with Western countries and the United Nations to help with infrastructure along with the work already being done by China

Men and Women of God who love the Lord will serve and worship Him without wavering in the most humble places throughout Congo

In addition to the quarter of a million people who are part of the Mennonite denominations of Congo, you can find many other segments of the population who are living Godly lives thanks to the mission work of other churches and denominations. One example of this exists in the eastern part of Congo, under the WEC (Worldwide Evangelization for Christ) leadership. There are hundreds more that provide both the bread of life and the necessities of life through the work of missionaries from the 20th Century. They worship several times a week in churches just like the one pictured below, with no roof and partial walls.

When the world's perception of Congo becomes more positive!

What is hard to understand for those who have never been to Congo is that there is a wonderful positive spirit in places that most of us would never survive. Once you see and experience that attitude, it is impossible to not think that someday, this country and this people will be considered to be one of the elite places in the world! Thankfully, there are many sources of information available today to help form a more complete understanding of the wonderful people who are citizens of Congo. The most important ingredient is for more people to meet the optimistic Congolese in person.

The viewers of the CBS news show, *60 Minutes* got a glimpse of this incredible optimism when they discovered the Congolese Symphony Orchestra a few years back. (We have included clips from that script)

The following script is from "*Joy in the Congo*" which aired on April 8, 2012. Bob Simon is the correspondent. Clem Taylor and Magalie Laguerre, producers.

Beauty has a way of turning up in places where you'd least expect it. We went to the Congo a few weeks ago, the poorest country in the world. Kinshasa, the capital, has a population of

10 million and almost nothing in the way of hope or peace. But there's a well-kept secret down there. Kinshasa has a symphony orchestra, the only one in Central Africa, the only all-black one in the world.

It's called the Kimbanguist Symphony Orchestra. We'd never heard of it. No one we called had ever heard of it. But when we got there we were surprised to find 200 musicians and vocalists, who've never played outside Kinshasa, or have been outside Kinshasa. We were even more surprised to find joy in the Congo. When we told the musicians they would be on *60 Minutes*, they didn't know what we were talking about but, still, they invited us to a performance.

We caught up with them as they were preparing outside their concert hall, a rented warehouse. As curtain time neared, we had no idea what to expect. But maestro Armand Diangienda seemed confident and began the evening with bang.

The music, Carmina Burana, was written by German composer Carl Orff 75 years ago. Did he ever dream that it would be played in the Congo? It wouldn't have been if it hadn't been for Armand and a strange twist of fate. Armand was a commercial pilot until 20 years ago when his airline went bust. So, like ex-pilots often do, he decided to put together an orchestra. He was missing a few things.

Bob Simon: You had no musicians, you had no teachers, you had no instruments.

Armand Diangienda: Yes.

Bob Simon: And you had no one who knew how to read music?

Armand Diangienda: No, nobody. Nobody.

Armand's English is limited. He preferred speaking French, Congo's official language.

Bob Simon: When you started asking people if they wanted to be members of this orchestra, did they have any idea what you were talking about?

Translation for Armand Diangienda: In the beginning, he said, people made fun of us, saying here in the Congo classical music puts people to sleep.

(You are reading correctly, they made almost all of their instruments out of junk that if we found on the street would be discarded. More dialogue from the *Joy of the Congo*)

And this is how they get to rehearsal. Six days a week, 90 minutes each way. Some would call it a trek. For them, it's a commute. When they get downtown, the last stretch is on a bus. What keeps them going? The music, always the music.

Sabine Kallhammer: They come here every day. They sing, and they go home. It's really amazing.

Bob Simon: It's pretty difficult to relate to that, isn't it?

Sabine Kallhammer: Yeah. Yeah. I don't think that anybody would do that with these conditions, in our country, no.

The boys and the choir have quite a repertoire now: Bach, Mendelssohn, Handel and, of course, Beethoven. The week we were there, the orchestra was rehearsing Beethoven's Ninth Symphony. Not exactly starter music, but Armand was determined to take it on and, like a good general, he reviewed all his troops.

The choir, OK. The strings? Not bad. But the full orchestra? Not quite.

French horns, he said, "You're hitting it too hard..."

"Be mindful of the echo", he told the string section.

Finally, it all came together and on the night of the performance, in this rented warehouse, Beethoven came alive. It's called the Ode to Joy, the last movement of Beethoven's last symphony. It has been played with more expertise before...but with more joy? Hard to imagine.

(The orchestra was invited to go to Europe to play with other orchestras in 2012)

Music brings us all together!

If there is a lesson you can learn from the Congolese people it is the joy of music. Lodema had to learn the hard way that containing the natural joy that comes from a tradition of music among the Congolese people is a mistake. She wanted the kids in her choir to hit the right notes and to make sure the harmony was being heard from all the voices in the choir, but the kids also wanted to take that harmony to levels that were not written into the readable music.

At first she thought this to be an affront to her authority and she even stalked out of church one day when she thought the kids were doing this intentionally to upset her. She came to find out that the kids could take a song and move it from a well-executed piece of music or hymn into an expression of passion and love for the Lord. They would do that using the same musical and rhythmic traditions that are part of their heritage.

Once she was able to understand that the balance between formal musical skills and the passionate expression of joy that translates from the soul of the people, she realized the value of both. Of all the ingredients that offer optimism, music must be at the top of the list of activities that play a role in both daily life as well as worship. Lodema was also able to see this value to music when she played the organ in her house that she was able to ship over to Africa. Both the missionary families and many of her Congolese students would enjoy the sounds that came out of her heart and her home from the organ music in Nyanga.

Women's choir from Djoko Punda; Tshikapa (Photo by author, July, 2012)

We also observed this same passion for music during the Centennial Celebration in 2012 when a choral group of twenty young women and five men from Djoko Punda, WALKED OVER ONE HUNDRED MILES, to sing at the events in Tshikapa. As you see these young women pictured above, you should know that three of them also had babies less than one year of age. One of the traditions that this choir taught the Americans was how to take up the offering. In Congo they do not pass an offering plate around. Each person responds as they feel the Spirit and "dance" forward to the offering basket to share their money as a cheerful giver. One of our members thought we would see larger gifts if we copied that idea.

This same indomitable spirit is what will make a difference in Congo for generations to come. If they can turn junk into musical instruments, and walk hundreds of miles to share their talent, they can also move the Congo forward! When a mutual respect for women in society and the leaders of the country unite under a spirit of honesty and integrity, there will be a new day in Congo! When people adopt the same fervor for their country as they have for the Lord's work in the church, Congo will find a new source of energy for their country. The missionaries of Congo did return after Independence, and the model they left behind fostered a strong dedicated church in many parts of the country. That same legacy will be sufficient for the country as a whole if the people will turn to God and turn their lives to Him for their vision and guidance.

Momma Kanemu's Legacy

"There are different kinds of gifts, but the same Spirit. There are different kinds of service, but the same Lord. There are different kinds of working, but the same God works all of them in all men (women)." I Corinthians 12:4-6(NIV)

"Do you think I am beautiful?"

In 2012, the Congolese Mennonite Churches celebrated one hundred years of a Christian witness in the Kasai Region of the Democratic Republic of Congo. More than 60 people shared in interviews about their relationship with Lodema Short nee Momma Kanemu. One of the pastors, Mardone Kachingu, related that his future depended on an oral exam that he had to pass in order to enter the University for teachers at Nyanga. Lodema was one of the three members of the academic board that were asking him questions and holding his fate in their hands. He had tried to prepare for the most difficult questions he could imagine when Lodema asked him, "Do you think I am beautiful?"

Clearly in his mind, he was certain that he did not want to give a quick or flip "yes" or "no" to such a question so he started to redefine the word beautiful and work around rationalizations while trying to figure out why she threw that question at him during this kind of exam. The missionary from Archbold, Ohio, who had been single all of her life, and to most people's knowledge never even had a serious boyfriend, gave this young student no more than a few minutes before she burst out in laughter at his stumbling and rambling answer to her mind numbing question. He was most relieved that she had such a sense of humor and also allowed him to see how he would respond to the unexpected.

Pastor Kachingu did pass the interview and eventually became a pastor and teacher. But, what about the answer to Lodema's question? How would you have answered such a question? After several years of study and research, I can answer Lodema's question, **YES YOU ARE BEAUTIFUL!!!**

You were beautiful when you took the extra time to help the kids at Spiess School near Archbold to learn their lessons in a one room school house while encouraging your nephew to work hard and grow stronger in his studies.

You were beautiful when you gave your heart to Jesus and responded to His calling in your life to become a full time servant of the Lord, and to go to Moody Bible Institute to study, and follow your calling to the mission field.

You were beautiful when you heard Archie and Irma Graber share their testimony and stories about the Belgian Congo at your home church in Archbold and you opened your heart to the possibility of joining them.

You were beautiful when you would be a unifying force in your own family and friends by bringing them together and keeping them informed of your hopes and dreams. Not just with your brothers Laurel and Fred, and sister Isabelle, but their spouses and children were also inspired and influenced for their lives by your life decisions. Even the next generation of great and multiple great nieces and nephews will know just how beautiful your dedication and passion for service to others carried you to places that they can only dream about.

You were beautiful when you would show kindness to the other missionary kids (MK's) by serving them fancy meals and inviting them to your house where the only organ could be found in that part of Congo. They were always impressed by your touches of home with lace table clothes and napkins that looked like a first class restaurant. They lived a lifetime of service themselves as they learned to live with less than their counterparts who never had to leave the comforts and advantages of life in North America. You were able to make them feel special knowing that they were missing something, but they never missed feeling the joy of good food in their stomach thanks to your endless sources of goodies from those silver barrels of surprise ingredients from your USA support team.

You were beautiful when you demanded the kids show up on time for class. They not only never forgot it; they were able to implement that same discipline in their ministries and classrooms when they became the person in charge. Four part harmony is a lost art for many but you can line up your former students and they all will sing their part because you cared enough to teach them how to read and write music in addition to feeling it and expressing it through their heritage. Your students will forever remember to ask tough questions and expect high performance because you expected it from them.

You were beautiful when you returned home and re-connected with your family and friends in the USA as if four or five years had passed without any break in your relationship with everyone. Part of this is because you were a tireless correspondent by writing hundreds of letters to numerous family members who would share their current and future plans along with the important events in each life. How special it was to see you share your life with all of those relatives when your time on furlough was so limited.

You were beautiful when you would return after seven different terms to the mission field and each time find new roommates and house mates in the single women's home at each mission station. This constant challenge to place the calling and the task of each term's special needs above personal comforts and preferences made your presence a pleasure to be associated with by all of your colleagues.

You were beautiful when you agreed to help train and then chaperone the nine *Happy Singers* who went to Belgium representing the entire mission work of the Mennonite's of Congo in 1958. You were able to balance the need to keep a proper discipline in their performances, but also allow them to enjoy themselves in an environment that was as close to a modern wonderland for them as they would ever experience. That watershed event still resonates to this day as the descendants of each of those men and even the other members of their class understood the possibilities of the world beyond Congo. The greatest beauty of this experience was that they did not have to leave Congo to understand the largesse of God's creation, but when they did return, they could embrace the world in a whole new way.

You were beautiful when you understood the value and dignity of the students and their families in Congo. This was no small task considering the predominant point of view in the world, and even in the realm of missionaries. There was a theme of white people being superior and teaching the inferior people of a remote country like Congo. You helped to reverse that trend by first convincing the Congolese that they could do great things, and that they were also beautiful. It started with the respect that you were able to show the boys in school, and very soon it spread to having a similar respect for the girls. It meant that if you could see them as strong and capable students, they would see themselves that way.

You were beautiful when you realized this same respect would be important in carrying over to the leadership of the church. Not everyone was on board with the idea of turning all the controls over to the Congolese leaders as quickly as it took place. You were confident that God would call unique and strong leaders to serve the church because you had seen the same kind of strength of character in your students who were now the leaders in the church.

You were beautiful during the 1960 Evacuation when people enjoyed kidding you about your fishing boots. They were a fashion statement for sure, but you were also a little upset when they did not make it back to Congo when the cars were left in Angola. As far as we know, you left the deeper water fishing to others after that loss.

You were beautiful when you brought a larger worldly perspective to your students. Beyond all the discipline and respect that they had for you, they also were able to find a sense of importance to explore ideas and areas of study that went beyond their own experience. Competence in their studies or getting art supplies was just step one in your vision for them, while understanding and interpretation were close allies in your desire for their growth. Many of them confirm that very presence in their lives as teachers, pastors, and parents.

You were beautiful in your sense of service. We could see this of course in your willingness to go to the Belgian Congo in 1947; but also to return again just two years after the Evacuation. But during and in between, you would take on extra roles in the churches in Nyanga, Archbold, Brussels, or wherever God had called you. It was this lesson you taught all of us best. First, get right with God, then follow His leading in all aspects of your life; then you will be at peace. Indeed, you will feel as close to being home here in this world as is possible until we are at **Home** with God in heaven. We look forward to seeing you there!

Appendix A - The Missionary Team

This book is dedicated to all those who have served or are serving in Congo or other African countries where CIM/AIMM are engaged. We have attempted to list as many as we know but acknowledge & apologize that some may be missed. God knows all who served even better and we trust that will be in their crown.

Those who served the Congo Inland Mission (CIM later to become the Africa Inter-Mennonite Missions (AIMM). (Data compiled through 1998 by Jim Bertsche in, *CIM/AIMM, A Story Of Vision, Commitment and Grace.*)

The time span listed also includes furloughs

Wayne & Annette (Jost) Albrecht	5/72 to 12/74
Milton & Beulah (MacMillen) Amie	8/28 to 4/32
Oscar & Sarah (Kroeker) Anderson	7/14 to 11/16
Hulda (Banman) Thiessen	5/56 to 7/71 (three terms)
Harvey & Avril (Reimer) Barkman	6/58 to 6/72 (three terms)
John P. & Mathilda (Stuckey) Barkman	3/16 to 9/45 (four terms)
Sue Barkman	1973 to 1976
Alvin & Martha (Foster) Becker	11/23 to 2/35 (two terms)
Irma Breitler (later married Archie Graber)	8/48 to 4/51
David Bergen	6/83 to 7/85
Phil & Carol (Kliewer) Bergen	9/90 to 6/2000+ (three terms)
Richard & Adela (Sawatzky) Bergen	1/85 to 7/2000+ (two terms)
Amelia Bertsche	8/20 to 9/31 (two terms)
James & Genevieve (Shuppert) Bertsche	7/48 to 8/86 (eight terms)
Sandra Bertsche	8/75 to 7/28 (two terms)
Timothy & Laura (Gilbertson) Bertsche	1/85 to 8/99 (four terms)

Erma Birky	4/23 to 6/60 (five terms)
Lester and Alma (Diller) Bixel	11/21 to 2/30 (two terms)
Glen & Phyllis (Thomas) Boese	1/84 to 7/92 (four terms)
John & Tina (Warkentin) Bohn	8/63 to 6/93 (seven terms combined)
Robert & Mable (Busch) Bontrager	5/50 to 3/65 (three terms)
Bryan & Teresa (Toews) Born	6/92 to 1997+ (two terms)
Don Boschman & Kathleen Rempel-Boschman	9/85 to 5/97 (four terms)
Henry & Sara Jo (Lehman) Braun	12/70 to 3/72
Lois Braun	1/86 to 9/91 (two terms)
Clio Briggs	11/23 to 3/27
Maurice & Joyce (Suran) Briggs	9/84 to 5/92 (four terms)
Loyd & Marie (Diller) Brown	8/52 to 7/60 (two terms)
Victor Buck	1953 to 1958
Charles Buller	8/81 to 10/83
Herman & Ruth (Lehman) Buller	2/66 to 3/88 (six terms)
Peter & Gladys (Klassen) Buller	**8/51 to 3/93 (nine terms)**
Allen & Marabeth (Loewens) Busenitz	1/73 to 3/76
John & Martha (Beiler) Byler	8/63 to 11/97 (five terms)
James & Cheryl (LeRoy) Campbell	9/81 to 3/84 (two terms)
Cheryl Cecil	1994 to 1998+
James & Jeanette (Myers) Christensen	6/78 to 8/84 (two terms)
Gordon & Jarna (Rautakoski) Claassen	9/83 to 12/93 (three terms)
Melvin & Martha (Buhler) Claassen	3/58 to 6/74 (four terms)
Donna Colbert	8/79 to 3/87 (four terms)
Troy & Cathy (Schmitz) Couillard	9/90 to 7/91
Doris Countryman	2/36 to 4/37
Linda Cummings	1/88 to 9/93 (two terms)
Harlan & Claire (Becker) deBrun	8/83 to 4/86
Rick & Marilyn (Carter) Derksen	6/76 to 7/98 (seven terms)
Norman & Virginia (Martin) Derstine	6/76 to 7/78
Delbert & Susan (Mast) Dick	7/75 to 1/94 (four terms)
Elmer & Esther (Quiring) Dick	**1/46 to 5/90 (nine terms)**
LaVerna Dick	8/72 to 7/76

James & Jeanne (Miller) Diller	9/56 to 6/60
Henry & Tina (Weier) Dirks	**8/63 to 5/98 (11 terms)**
Rudy & Sharon (Andres) Dirks	7/96 to 1999+
Alma Doering	2/23 to 12/25
Harry & Lois (Riehl) Dyck	8/75 to 1/97 (three terms)
Sarah Dyck	5/56 to 2/58
Mr. Edghart	1/16 to 10/16
Sam & Honora (Fast) Ediger	11/52 to 8/57
James & Vicki (Birkey) Egli	9/80 to 10/83
Ben & Helen (Reimer) Eidse	10/53 to 12/82 (six terms)
Bill & Betty (Giesbrecht) Enns	6/95 to 1999+
Frank & Agnes (Neufeld) Enns	**10/26 to 7/69 (seven terms)**
Lorin & Sandra (Barkman) Enns	8/75 to 8/77
Loren & Donna (Kampen) Entz	9/77 to 1998+ (six terms+)
Sam & Leona (Enns) Entz	11/49 to 11/75 (five terms)
Mary Epp	**6/58 to 8/87 (nine terms)**
Ralph & Fern (Bartsch) Ewert	8/61 to 8/78 (three terms)
Peter & Annie (Rempel) Falk	**8/52 to 7/87 (seven terms)**
Eric & Kathleen (Harms) Fast	7/87 to 8/94
Charles Fennig	3/81 to 8/83
Jerome & Ramona Fluth	7/95 to 8/96
John & Betty (Rempel) Franz	6/73 to 7/75
Aganetha K. Friesen	**9/38 to 10/74 (five terms)**
Donald & Norma (Klassen) Friesen	1/82 to 12/84
Irvin & Lydia (Gunther) Friesen	11/76 to 4/86 (three terms)
Ivan & Rachel (Hilty) Friesen	12/86 to 6/92 (two terms)
Lena K. Friesen	7/51 to 7/60 (two terms)
Margaret Friesen	7/57 to 6/60
Rick & June (Ashton) Friesen	9/86 to 7/90
Sandra Friesen	9/83 to 6/89 (two terms)
Sara K. Friesen	7/51 to 7/60 (two terms)
Anne Garber	9/75 to 1/93 (four terms)
Ellis & Edna (Buller) Gerber	9/53 to 7/73 (six terms)
Robert & Joyce (Stradinger) Gerhart	10/74 to 8/88 (three terms)

Virgil & Mary Kay (Ramseyer) Gerig	3/82 to 7/84
Archie & Evelyn (Oyer) Graber	**5/30 to 4/51 (four terms)**
Archie & Irma (Beitler) Graber	**4/51 to 4/73 (six terms)**
Nancy Graber Roth	**8/83 to 10/85**
Harold & Gladys (Gjerdevig) Graber	1/51 to 6/64 (three terms)
John & Betty (Stover) Grasse	4/86 to 11/90 (two terms)
Gary & Maureen (Penner) Groot	9/83 to 5/86
Max & Ruth (Germann) Grutter	1955 to 1956
Frieda Guengerich	1/46 to 11/74 (five terms)
Titus & Karen (Loewen) Guenther	9/81 to 6/84
Theresa Gustafson	2/23 to 4/31 (two terms)
Klara Gut	10/55 to 10/56
Marlene Habegger	1991 to 1997
Lawrence & Rose (Boehning) Haigh	**4/11 to 6/20 (two terms;**
FIRST MISSIONARIES FROM THE MENNONITE CONFERENCE TO SETTLE IN CONGO)	
Archie & Ella Haller	9/25 to 8/27
Elvira Hamm	7/96 to 1999+
Wade Handrich	10/95 to 1999+
Arnold & Grace (Hiebner) Harder	**10/68 to 4/92 (nine terms +**
special assignments for the Centennial Celebration)	
Judith Harder	9/85 to 6/89 (two terms)
Steven & Judith (Dickerson) Harder	1/85 to 5/87
Waldo & Abbie (Claassen) Harder	7/51 to 6/73 (four terms)
Harold & Joyce (Ediger) Harms	8/59 to 6/68 (three terms)
Mary Hendershott	1995 to 1999+
Walter Scott Herr	11/12 to 6/17
Steve Hershberger	1990 to 1995
Elda Hiebert	8/63 to 7/91 (five terms)
Mary Hiebert	4/57 to 3/66 (two terms)
Henry & Hilda (Klassen) Hildebrand	8/58 to 7/61 (two terms)
Laurence Hills	9/82 to 5/89 (three terms)
Richard & Jean (Simpson) Hirschler	4/71 to 12/84 (three terms)
Fiona Holburn	1995 to 1999+

Gary & Jean (Kliewer) Isaac	10/86 to 1999+ (six terms)
Marvin & Edna (Mays) Isaac	8/67 to 7/71
John & Ann (Dick) Jantzen	8/49 to 8/59 (two terms)
Arthur & Martini (Reimer) Janz	**12/51 to 12/94 (eight terms)**
Aaron & Ernestine Janzen	11/12 to 11/21 (two terms)
Anita Janzen	8/67 to 6/80 (three terms)
Garry & Diane (Janzen) Janzen	9/85 to 8/88
Frederick Johnstone	7/14 to 4/17
Henning & Elsie (Lundberg) Karlson	6/16 to 6/18
Sofi Karlson	1/16 to 7/17
Cheri Keefer	9/71 to 8/73
Levi & Eudene (King) Keidel 3/51 to 5/81 (five terms)	
Ruth Keidel	**7/78 to 6/80**
William & Edna (Moser) Kensinger	1/19 to 9/25 (two terms)
John & Olga (Unruh) Klaassen	8/64 to 9/76
Gordon & Rebecca (Balzer) Klassen	9/90 to 6/98 (two terms)
John & Ruth (Fast) Kliewer	5/78 to 9/81
Henry & Phyllis Klopfenstein	3/23 to 5/26
Daniel & Anne (Garber) Kompaore	8/93 to 1999+ (two terms+)
Glen & Elizabeth (Unger) Koop	9/90 to 7/92
John & Leona (Bergen) Krause	11/78 to 8/83 (two terms)
Ronald & Cynthia (Kirchofer) Krehbiel	8/78 to 7/79
Mr. & Mrs. B.F. Langdon	10/23 to 9/25
Jonathon & Mary Kay (Burkhalter) Larson	7/81 to 11/94 (four terms)
Vernon & Phyllis (Lehman) Lehman	2/77 to 8/79
Anna V. Liechty	**4/46 to 7/84 (nine terms)**
Irena Liechty	**7/52 to 5/62 (three terms, see**
Sprunger)	
Henry & Betty (Schroeder) Loewen	8/72 to 7/80 (two terms)
Melvin & Elfrieda (Regier) Loewen	8/55 to 6/67 (four terms)
Lorraine Lowenberg	1964 to 1969
Agnes Lutke	4/46 to 6/60 (three terms)
Berta Mangold	1954 to 1958
Darrell & Diana (Crane) Mann	8/67 to 1/69

Rudolph & Elvina (Neufeld) Martens	8/52 to 5/80 (five terms)
Anna Meester	3/15 to 4/18
Anne Merkey	1978 to 1979
Bertha Mae Miller	**2/29 to 12/69 (five terms)**
Mary Miller	2/29 to 7/57 (four terms)
Tracy Moschel	1989 to 1990
Henry & Emma (Bixler) Moser	2/23 to 7/46 (four terms)
Gordon & Kathryn (Graber) Myers	9/85 to 6/88
Stephen & Patricia (Wicke) Nelson	8/84 to 8/93 (three terms)
Cindy Neuenschwander	1993 to 1998
Marjorie Neuenschwander	8/72 to 7/85 (three terms)
Wilbert & Ruby (Moser) Neuenschwander	7/64 to 8/73 (two terms)
George & Justina (Wiens) Neufeld	11/44 to 7/69 (four terms)
Gerald & Beverly (Dueck) Neufeld	9/87 to 1999+ (six terms)
Rachel Nolt	1997 to 1999+
Stan & Lorri (Berends) Nussbaum	3/77 to 1999+ (five terms)
John & Mary (Schrag) Pauls	8/80 to 6/83
Mary Penner	12/68 to 4/70
Daniel & Kathy (Fluth) Petersen	9/82 to 1999+ (four terms)
Stephen & Janet (Sinclair) Plenert	9/86 to 1999+ (four terms)
Anna Quiring	4/36 to 12/58 (four terms)
Betty Quiring	7/54 to 10/79 (seven terms)
Tina Quiring	10/49 to 7/76 (five terms)
Doreen Ratzlaff	1979 to 1988
Glenn & Pauline (Gima) Rediger	7/88 to 9/91 (two terms)
Arnold & Elaine (Waltner) Regier	8/57 to 7/60
Elmer & Gloria (Bridson) Regier	7/56 to 5/60
Fremont & Sara (Janzen) Regier	1/64 to 7/85 (five terms)
Amanda Reimer	8/53 to 7/60 (two terms)
Brian & Patricia (Penner) Reimer	8/92 to 6/97 (two terms)
Dennis & Jeanne (Sonke) Rempel	1/78 to 7/86 (three terms)
Eldora Rempel	1952 to 1958
Erwin & Angela (Albrecht) Rempel	6/94 to 1999+ (two terms)
Lawrence & Alvera (Klassen) Rempel	8/48 to 8/71 (five terms)

Emma Rickert	2/23 to 6/28 (two terms)
Evelyn Riediger	1/85 to 11/85
Dennis & Shirley (Epp) Ries	11/75 to 7/84 (three terms)
Glenn & Ina (Rowell) Rocke	**6/46 to 10/84 (ten terms)**
David & Catherine (Bear) Rocke	**3/77 to 6/80**
Earl & Ruth (Jantzen) Roth	**7/54 to 8/93 (eight terms)**
Lynn & Kathleen (Brandt) Roth	8/85 to 5/89 (two terms)
Jeanette Rupp	1949 to 1951
Mabel Sauder	1/38 to 6/52 (two terms)
Peter & Marge Sawatzky	9/79 to 7/80
Ronald D. Sawatzky	8/77 to 7/89 (six terms)
Christine Schaeper	10/55 to 10/56
John & Charity (Eidse) Schellenberg	8/86 to 12/89
Fanny Schmallenberger	2/35 to 7/72 (six terms)
Bonnie Schmidt	7/95 to 7/97
Dennis & Dianne (Smith) Schmidt	8/80 to 7/87 (two terms)
Loyal & Donna (Williams) Schmidt	3/54 to 7/64 (five terms)
Robert & Joyce (Williams) Schmidt	8/69 to 12/72
Russell & Helen (Yoder) Schnell	**11/32 to 5/64 (five terms)**
Leona Schrag	**8/68 to 1999+ (six terms)**
Grace Schram	9/25 to 8/27
Merle & Dorothy (Bowman) Schwartz	**3/41 to 3/77 (nine terms)**
Kay Frances Sharping	1970 to 1973
Walter & Elizabeth (Bauman) Shelly	6/68 to 7/77 (three terms)
Linda Short	1976 to 1978
Lodema Short	**4/47 to 4/81 (nine terms)**
Rhoda Short	1969 to 1970
Lois V. Slagle	**4/45 to 8/77 (seven terms)**
Paul & Martine (Ehrismann) Solomiac	1984 to 1999+ (two terms)
Mr. & Mrs. Emil Sommer	7/17 to 3/32 (four terms)
Agnes Sprunger	**3/16 to 8/53 (six terms)**
Charles & Geraldine (Reiff) Sprunger	7/57 to 6/72 (four terms)
Jeanette Sprunger	1961
Vernon & Lilly (Liechty) Sprunger	6/62 to 11/72 (four terms)

Wilmer & Kenlyn (Augsburger) Sprunger 7/65 to 7/73 (two terms)

James & Mary Ellen (Wolber) Steiner 9/68 to 9/70

Richard & Gladys (Cleveland) Steiner 8/85 to 6/98 (four terms)

Alvin J. Stevenson 2/12 to 2/13

Bill & Sally (Cadwallader) Stieglitz 9/97 to 1999+

David & Elvera (Dyck) Stoesz 7/93 to 6/95

Helen Stoesz 10/26 to 3/36 (two terms)

Marvin & Dorothy (Leu) Storrer 8/66 to 6/69

Omar & Laura (Becker) Sutton 5/23 to 11/42 (three terms)

Mathew & Rebecca (Jackson) Swora 8/85 to 7/88

Elmer & Jeannette (Dueck) Thiessen 8/86 to 1999+ (three terms)

Erica Thiessen 2/91 to 6/97 (three terms)

Paul & Lois (Fast) Thiessen 9/83 to 1999+ (four terms)

Eugene Thieszen 8/92 to 1999+ (two terms)

Helen Thieszen 11/30 to 9/33

Russell & Gail (Wiebe) Toevs 9/81 to 2/91 (three terms combined)

G. Tolefson 1/16 to 10/16

Henry & Naomi (Zacharius) Unrau 7/78 to 6/86 (three terms)

Kornelia Unrau **3/26 to 6/60 (five terms)**

Donovan & Naomi (Reimer) Unruh 10/68 to 8/87 (five terms)

Rudolph Unruh 9/31 to 3/36

Selma Unruh 4/46 to 1/64 (four terms)

Mr. & Mrs. Raphael Valentine 2/23 to 9/25

Susan Wagler 9/82 to 4/84

Harris & Christine (Duerksen) Waltner 7/84 to 7/90 (two terms)

Edwin & Irene (Lehman) Weaver 1/75 to 8/79 (two terms)

Meta Weith 2/23 to 7/26

Allan & Selma (Schmidt) Wiebe 8/50 to 2/61 (two terms)

Donna Yoder 1958 to 1961

James & Linda (Bertsche) Yoder 9/82 to 9/85

Roy & Bessie (Burns) Yoder 4/35 to 1/50 (three terms)

John & Jeanne (Pierson) Zook 8/55 to 11/97 (seven terms)

(Highlights indicate missionaries who spent thirty or more years in service)

Appendix B - The Volunteer Workers

Voluntary Service Personnel who have served with CIM/AIMM in Congo and other parts of Africa. This list is a compilation from Jim Bertsche's work in **"CIM/AIMM: A Story of Vision Commitment and Grace,"** and is dated from 1998. We apologize if we missed anyone and acknowledge that we recognize all who served. Many of the people you will see on this list volunteered to give themselves and their time to this cause. Others were offering their services as an alternative to military service and their efforts to promote education, agriculture, construction, mechanics, transportation, medical services, public health, and many specialty projects all contributed to the delivery of the Gospel.

Art & Clara Augsburger
Art & Frieda Banman
Harlan Bartel
Elmer Beachy
Gertrude Bergen
Peter & Anne Bergen
Steven Boese
Wilbur Bontrager
Kris & Jill Bullock
Jan Bundy Krehbiel
Mary Burkholder
Roger Busenitz
Ronald & Gloria Camp
Edward Rosemay Charles
David Claassen

Susan Clifton

Alvin Dahl

Albert & Annie Drudge

Anna Ediger

Sam & Betty Ediger

Soloman & Lavina Ediger

Elena Entz

Loren Entz

Russell Entz

Dale Epp

Maureen Fink

Katherine Fountain

Mildred Freeman

Aden & Sheryl Frey

Anne Garber

Amber Gates

Larry Geisinger

Ann Getrz

Henry Gerbrandt

Henry Goertz

Larry Graber

John Heese

Nancy Heisey

Leslie Hertzler

Wilbur & Elizabeth Hershberger

Charles Hieb

Paul Hodel

Dennis Holsopple

Allen Horst

John Janzen

Larry Kauffman

Merle Kauffman

Melvin Keim

Andrea Kellerstrass

Brenda Klassen

Angela Lehman

David Lehman

Verney Lehrman

Ed & Ada Liechty

Gordon & Minda Liechty

Dean Linsenmeyer

Don & Mary Lloyd

Karen Maughan

Darrell Martin

Raymond & Ruth Milhous

Ron Mininger

Willie Neuenschwander

Alfred Neufeldt

Arnold & Lorene Nickel

James Peters

Arlo & Leontina Raid

Fremont Regier

Paul Rempel

Phil & Gwen Rich

David Ritter

Paul Roth

Bob Rounds

Beverly Sawatzky Martens

Charis Schellenberg

Lisa Schellenberg

Les Schlegel

Loyal Schmidt

Olin & Tillie Schmidt

Robert Schmidt

Jeffrey & Nancy Shear

Joe Shetler

Alan Siebert

Wilmer Sprunger

Sonja Strahm
Terry Stuckey
Abe Suderman
Fred Suter
Margaret Sweebe
Bernard Thiessen
Rose Thiessen Neufeld
Mary Tretheway
Henry Unrau
Donovan Unruh
Janinne Unruh
Larry Unruh
Adrian Voran
Mark Weaver
Lloyd Wiebe
Ernest Yoder
Galen Yoder
Stan Yoder
Martha Yoder Maust
James & Leanne Zacharias
Greg Zimmerman

To the hundreds of pastors and volunteers in all of the churches that the missionaries and volunteers represented, we salute your time, efforts, and dedication to fund raising and building awareness for your congregations of the challenges that the people were facing in Congo. For the financial support that was given from sacrificial budgets knowing that the work of those in Congo would not come back void, we also send a special dedication and thanks for your contribution in the telling of this story. Blessings to you as you help even today in those mission projects that need your time, talent, and treasure.

Bibliography

(Sources used by the author as well as publications recommended for others who wish to research topics related to the Congo and its history)

Selling the Congo, by Matthew Stanard (Article from 2005 European History Quarterly, "The 1958 Brussels World's Fair and Belgian Perceptions of the Congo")

C.T. Studd, Cricketer & Pioneer, by Norman Grubb (donated by Peter Conway)

War To Be One, by Levi O. Keidel

Caught in the Crossfire, by Levi Keidel

Heart of Darkness, by Joseph Conrad

King Leopold's Ghost by Adam Hochschild

The Scramble For Africa, by Thomas Pakenham (recommended by Tom Lynch)

To God Be The Glory, by Margaret Lovick (donated by Glenn & Hyacinth Smith)

The Congo from Leopold To Kabila, A People's History, by Georges Nzongola-Ntalaja

Coltan, by Michael Nest

Consuming The Congo, War & Conflict Minerals in the World's Deadliest Place, by Peter Eichstaedt

Called to Mission, Mennonite Women Missionaries In Central Africa in the Second Half of the 20th Century, by Mirjam Rahel Scarborough

In The Footsteps of Mr. Kurtz, On the Brink of Disaster in Mobutu's Congo, by Michela Wrong

The Jesus Tribe, Grace stories from Congo's Mennonites from 1912 to 2012, by A Project of Africa Inter-Mennonite Missions

Africa, A Biography of the Continent, by John Reader

The Fate of Africa, A History of Fifty Years of Independence, by Martin Meredith

CIM/AIMM, A Story of Vision & Commitment & Grace, by Jim Bertsche

The Congo Messenger & Africa Journal, Newsletters from over fifty years by CIM/AIMM

African Perspectives on Colonialism, by A. Adu Boahen

Congo Masquerade, by Theodore Trefon

Dancing in the Glory of Monsters, by Jason K. Stearns

Africa, Altered States, Ordinary Miracles, by Richard Dowden

About the Author

Dwight Short was visiting the Central Africa Museum in Tervuren just outside of Brussels in 2009 along with his American mission partner to France, Mike Zaubi. The artifacts looked familiar because his family had been the recipient of similar items when his Aunt Lodema returned from the Belgian Congo from her work in Africa, and shared them with all of her family. The symbols of Belgian colonial rule were apparent to him in every room of the museum. Finally, he discovered a room that gave some credence to the import and gravity of the influence that mission groups had brought to the Congolese people. This included the legacy of literacy thru the schools; basic health facilities thru clinics; and agricultural productivity thru advanced techniques of plant and animal husbandry.

Dwight could see his aunt and all of her colleagues in this small accommodation to the missionary influence in the Belgian museum. As he explained what he already knew about this to Mike, it was clear that the time to tell this story more clearly was quickly vanishing as the people who were students of this mission group would not be living much longer to tell this story first hand. It may have been Mike's words, "You have to go back to Nyanga where your aunt was teaching and find some of those kids!" Or, it may have been the fact that the museum continued to understate the value of all of the missionaries who had given their lives to better the lives of the Congolese people. It may also have been that the primary calling of all of those who gave their lives to this cause was to see more people hear and accept the Gospel message that moved the author to take the time to tell this story.

As the research and interviews started in early 2010, Jim Bertsche became the "go to" source for all of the questions about how these stories materialized. He suggested that visiting Congo with the Centennial Team in 2012 would be a priceless experience for him and for the readers of this book. Rod Hollinger-Janzen, the head of AIMM, and the leader of the team, also agreed that such a presence on the team would not be a distraction, and in fact would be another focal point for the heritage of the ministry and church in Congo.

As word spread throughout the Tshikapa area that Momma Kanemu's nephew was in the area and wanted to meet and talk with her former students, they came from everywhere. For seven days in July, 2012, the students (now in their sixties and seventies) just kept showing up to share their story of how Lodema and all of her mission partners had made all the difference in their lives. The prayer is that this story will have a similar impact on all who read, *Home Is Where God Calls Us.*

Dwight has spent over thirty four years as a financial advisor with Merrill Lynch; written books on Biblically Responsible Investing; helped to lead numerous sports mission trips; and provided leadership to many Christian organizations and churches. All of those activities were important preparation for this project. What began as a legacy project for his family, is now a teaching opportunity for those who have never heard about God's work in south central Congo.

Austin Brothers Publishing is a small publishing company that specializes in helping writers realize their dream of publishing a book. We can assist in any part of the process from having little more than an idea all the way to actually fulfilling orders for your printed book. As an author, you will work directly with editors and designers so the final product is a true reflection of what you intended. Our process is unique and allows the author to have a much greater share in the financial profit than with traditional publishers or other self-publishing models.

For more information visit our website –
www.austinbrotherspublishing.com

CPSIA information can be obtained at www.ICGtesting.com
Printed in the USA
LVOW01s0343150714

394379LV00002B/5/P